wreckage with a beating heart

Acknowledgements

"Humbled By Love" first appeared in *The Art of Dying* (Hohm Press, 1999).

"What I Saw Through the Hotel Window" first appeared in *Sho 1:2* (Spring 2003).

"Drinks Her Fill" first appeared in *The Atlanta Review* (Spring 2003).

"What the Assistant Professor Does Not Tell His Class" first appeared in *The Atlanta Review* (Tenth Anniversary Issue).

"The Farmer Plowing His Field" and "Men" first appeared in *Nimrod: International Journal of Poetry* 48:1 (Fall/Winter 2004).

"Beauty Is Dearest When It's Gone" first appeared in *The Bukowski Review* 3 (Spring/Summer 2004).

"The Bad Poet Sings" first appeared in *Gasping for Air In A Vacuum* (Lee Lozowick, Hohm Press, 2004).

"First You Have to Understand What the Problem Is" and "A Known Entity On the Poetry Scene" first appeared in *LocaList* 1:2 (September/October 2003).

"King Snake," "You May Think It Is Easy Being A Teacher," "The Cold Draft Beer," "The Leper," "Saint Moose," and "We Are Wreckage With A Beating Heart" first appeared in *Sho 1:1* (Spring 2002).

* * *

The cover art is "Entreaty," by Gary Simmons (pen & watercolor) of Hot Springs, Arkansas (please see last page for biographical information and artist's statement). This is our fourth book collaboration and i am deeply indebted to Gary for his generosity with his talent.

Author contact information: red hawk is available for readings, workshops, and lectures at: moorer@uamont.edu /824 N. Hyatt, Monticello, AR 71655

wreckage with a beating heart

"amo ergo sum"

poems by red hawk

Cover design: Gary Simmons
Layout and design: Kubera Services

Library of Congress Cataloging in Publication Data:
Red Hawk.
   Wreckage with a beating heart : "amo ergo sum" : poems / by Red Hawk.
ISBN 1-890772-50-X (pbk. : alk. paper)
1. Spiritual life--Poetry. I. Title.
 PS3568.E295W74 2005
   811'.54--dc22

                                           2005000765

                          HOHM PRESS
                          P.O. Box 2501
                       Prescott, AZ 86302
                         800-381-2700
                    http://www.hohmpress.com

This book was printed in the U.S.A. on acid-free paper using soy ink.

09 08 07 06 05   5 4 3 2 1

Dedication: jai Guru

To the Father, Yogi Ramsuratkumar: Heaven,
and to the Son, Mister Lee: Earth,
and to Osho, gone beyond Heaven and Earth.

For Gayle Maxene: Soul
and for Little Wind & Rain Drop: Heart.

For John Irwin & Tommy Logan: we are brothers with
    different mothers,
and for Joyce Elizabeth, Soul Sister.

Contents

Part ii. The Seeker: the middle world

Part iii. The Beggar: between 2 worlds

Part iv. The Master: the Angelic World

Prologue:

We Are Wreckage With A Beating Heart

We Are Wreckage With A Beating Heart

On fire we are burning things
thrust into the lime pit of life;
on fire we are drowning things
rising through the deep like breathing things
desperate for the killing air;
on fire we are
dying things dancing in the dark,
shadow beings stirring beneath root
and tuberous leafy moist dirt,
struggling, longing for Sunlight,
clawing through the spermy loam,
neighbor to the maggot and the potato grub,
the 7-year locust and the spider mite,
the Earthworm and the seed.

We are broken hearted wreckage with
a beating pulse, blood soaked beings
in love with our sorrows, the last hope,
the only chance, the roll of the dice
of Consciousness, Holy Nature
in a suit of burning flesh, the sperm,
the bloody egg fixed upon the uterine silk,
the naked need screaming for milk, the
loose canon, the random bullet fired
into the temple,
the balance sheet of an ignorant thief,
the marriage of flesh and the unseen
invisible passion,
the longing, the needing, the crying out

of God.
Do you imagine you inherit the bone,
the flesh, the thought and feeling,
the inchoate longing and despair
of the body?
You do not.
You inherit the doom of the flesh,
you inherit the invisible wantbone,
you inherit the blaze behind the eyes,
the infinite wandering, the wonder
and the kneel-down begging, the
complete surrender to a thing we cannot name,
the wreckage and the ruin, the constant
almighty breathing in and breathing out

of a Power which forever dies in splendid solitude
and is constantly reborn in helpless need.

Part i. The Fool: the underworld

"A fool is happy
Until his mischief turns against him.
And a good man may suffer
Until his goodness flowers...

But as dust thrown against the wind,
Mischief is blown back in the face
Of the fool who wrongs the pure and harmless...

...How long the wandering of many lives
To the fool who misses the Way...

The fool who knows he is a fool
Is that much wiser.
The fool who thinks he is wise
Is a fool indeed...

The fool is his own enemy.
The mischief he does is his undoing.
How bitterly he suffers!

> – Buddha, *The Dhammapada,* * 26–29, 45, 47

---

* All quotations from *The Dhammapada* are from the edition: Thomas Byrom,
Translator, New York: Alfred Knopf, 1976.

We Are All Babes In the Woods
(for Hayden)

Once we had common sense
because we were forced to live off the land
and have great respect for the elements.
Death was always close at hand

and we had to keep a watchful eye.
If a small child strayed too far from the compound
into the forest, before she could even make a cry
she would likely be found

by wolves or hungry bears.
Good sense has been replaced with machine:
because one man can plow a thousand acres
we think we are safe from famine;

because we have killed nearly every thing that moves,
we imagine we are safe from the wolves.

When the Clown is Dying

Richard Pryor once was a genuinely funny man
with the kind of insight into Human behavior
which only humor can deliver.
And then he came into the money,

lots of it, and that allowed him
to indulge his weaknesses;
it turns out his greatest fondness
was for the worst kind of drug,

free-base crack cocaine.
So today they are interviewing
on National Public Radio
the clown who was once touched by God.

He is torn apart and eaten alive
by the glass pipe.
He suffered third degree burns over
80% of his body while free-basing,

set himself on fire.
Now he has Multiple Sclerosis,
cannot walk, and often
can barely breathe.

He has trouble speaking.
He is asked how he has gotten through
such terrible times.
Free-based some coke, he says.

Do you still do it, they ask him?
Nope. I just quit recently,
he says.
Ahhh, the interviewer sighs,

ready at last amidst the horror
to report the miracle.
Did you have some revelation
she asks

which helped you quit?
Yeah, he says,
voice quivering like a
burned leaf still on the limb

after a fire has swept through,
I looked in my bank account
and it was
empty.

The Dog Catcher

Ronnie was older than the other boys in the
neighborhood and something was not quite right
with him; he was slow and mean, way behind
in school, held back 2-3 times. i blamed it all

on his father because he was the dog catcher.
Everyone hated him but
i used to go up there and watch him prepare
the meat. He had a big steel drum

full of rancid, stinking meat that he mixed
with poison and put in the back of his truck.
He drove down alleys and vacant lots, throwing
chunks of poison meat out for stray dogs.

He had a club in the truck; if he could lure a dog
with no collar close, he clubbed it, otherwise
he had a long pole in a rack on the truck's side.
It had a loop on one end and a rope attached

to the loop so when he looped the dog's neck he could
pull that rope and choke it so it couldn't run.
He took the bodies to the rendering plant on the
edge of town where they ground them into animal feed,

at least they said it was for the animals.
i think that's what broke Ronnie so he could
never be fixed, his old man killing all those dogs.
Spoiled his heart so it went bad like the meat

and like the dogs, Ronnie couldn't get away
from the dog catcher to save his life;
it's a mean dirty job and nothing
comes free here, nothing;

somebody always has to pay.

Why the Dog Is Man's Best Friend, Not Woman's

He will shit on the rug and never clean it up,
will live amidst unimaginable filth and
be quite happy, he only obeys

when given something to eat and
he will eat anything, no matter
what it is and where it has been;

he is only interested in others' butts and is
not too proud to plunge his nose into them
at first meeting if he is allowed,

and if the scent is to his liking
will immediately mount or hump
without foreplay until he is finished or rebuffed;

he is not ashamed to masturbate continuously,
even in front of others and when aroused,
which is often and easily, his only thought

is satisfaction at whatever cost, even
if that means dry-humping the leg
of the elderly, infirm or dead;

who else would be slavishly loyal to violent
lazy men, except a creature just like them
whose greatest delight

is drinking from a toilet?

First, You Have to Understand What the Problem Is

In the old days when you
walked into a sugar mill, the guard
at the gate had one hand, the watchman
and the broom pushers, the cleaning crew

were all one-handed men.
It made you wonder, until you came to
the extraction rollers, great metal or stone
drums where the sugar cane was ground

to extract the juice.
Timing was critical because the cane juice
spoiled quickly so at harvest
they milled the sugar cane around the clock

and the men feeding the rollers grew so tired
that their hands often slipped into the rollers
and if quick action was not taken
the whole arm and then the body

was drawn in.
For this purpose the mill owners, fat
rich men with large houses and clean clothes,
devised the perfect solution:

next to every set of drum rollers
a sharpened hatchet hung from a rope.
To the clean, fat, well-oiled men this
solved the problem.

Eureka!

i see a crazy man on the street and
he is shouting about the Rays, they are
everywhere.
People smile and keep on shuffling into
the stifling horror of their lives,
the endless treachery, the boredom
and they never suspect that the crazy one
knows more than they do because
he has made the leap, he is
crazy.
There are Rays everywhere of course,
we are bombarded by them: laser, radio,
TV, micro, electrical, gamma, alpha,
beta, short, ultra-violet, x, y, z
and we are as mad as he only
we don't shout on street corners, we just
kill each other in vast numbers or
ourselves one by one.
Everyone is looking for something, anything
to make some sense out of the madness
so we boast about our vaunted human intelligence,
strut it out as the thing which separates us from the
other lowly creatures of the Earth, point to men like
Archimedes who discovered the physics of volume displacement
when he lowered his body into a tub full of water
and the tub ran over; Eureka!
he shouted, and humans glow with pride
at this proof of their superiority, but
Pliny the Roman naturalist and

astute observer of the natural world,
500 years before Archimedes, tells
about a Raven he once saw
approach a narrow-neck vase with water in it
but the water wasn't high enough for him to reach so
he dropped pebbles into the vase
until its water level rose high enough
for him to get a drink.
So much for
human intelligence and
the discovery of the physics of volume displacement;
Eureka!
the rays, they are
everywhere.

The Insane Are Driving Each Other Crazy

My daughter does not want to hear the news
that everyone without exception is insane, not
in various stages of neurosis, not marginal
but certifiably locked up in the back ward and
fed through a tube
insane; she
berates me for making sweeping generalizations
because she cannot believe that
the president of the United States, the governor
of our state, the man in the cockpit of the 747,
the doctor doing brain surgery, the preacher,
the psychiatrist, the professor, the poet, the
movie star, the rock musician, the
whore, the pimp, the killer, the rapist, all
of us and your momma
are insane.

Oh sure,
i can tell you my name, i can
dress myself and i can talk the talk but
each of us in our own way is
driving everyone else crazy, we
use each other up, we burn each other out,
we suck and leech and bite and snarl
until it is all used up and we
blame it on love, we say
it was the full Moon, i had a bad childhood,
my mother was a drunk, my father
did this or that to me and he did it

over and over again but
the one thing we do not want to hear, the
one thing which neatly explains all of it at once
is that every single last quivering one of us is
locked in the basement, the attic or the broom closet,
drooling and peeing in our pants,
stumbling and fumbling and forgetting,
picking our noses and eating it,
deaf, dumb and blind, lost
and wandering the streets,
eating out of dumpsters, stockings
falling around our ankles, stains
in our underwear
insane.

What I Saw Through the Hotel Window

We are staying one night at the Ritz-Carlton
in Pasadena, way more than we can afford but
for one night i want my wife to be a queen,
she's worth it.
The bellman wears white gloves, the rich
lounge indifferently near the pool,
the stink of money hangs over us like the haze
over the burning ghats in India where the distinctions
between rich and poor are dissolved by fire.

I am sitting in our beautiful room
next to the window drinking wine when
to my horror and disbelief
a woman falls right past my window,
not plunges but floats on her back like
a slow motion movie, her hair flying
around her face, her arms straight out
like wings; she hovers there looking at me
and in an instant drops from sight.

My God! i yell.
What, my wife says. Nothing,
i say as the Thud! reaches the sixth floor
where i am standing, speechless.
F. Scott got it half-right, the very rich
are different from the rest of us:
they jump from
the most expensive
windows, but

they land just like you and me.

The Things We Do For Love

10 shot dead, 3 more wounded, the paper said.
One 12 year old was shot standing in the schoolhouse door;
he may live.
The snipers were a 40 year old man and his stepson who,
for whatever hell they came from, finally
had enough of failed love and went over the edge
where it is cold and lonely and
the world comes and hunts you down like a mad dog.
Once you go over that edge, you can
do anything and make it seem right.
The 2 of them prepared their old Chevy Caprice
for killing: they unbolted the back seat,
took the panel out that led into the trunk,
made it so a man with a high powered rifle
could stretch all the way out unseen, then
they cut a hole in the trunk,
a shooter's hole and
they set out for the suburbs of Maryland
looking to settle the scores
that the pain of love owed them.
Anything, so they could feel love together, the
stepson desperate for a father, the man
desperate to be one so he initiated his
willing boy in the rites of the assassin,
killing for love.
It is what we all do sooner or later,
we just don't use high powered rifles,
most of us; we figure out cleverer ways
to get away with murder.

You Don't Know What Love Is

On the way to the picnic I stop to buy
an apple pie and the big bag of corn chips,
my favorites.
We get there and drink beer, grill burgers
and have a good time.
Just to show what a good guy i am,
i leave them the rest of the apple pie
but i wrap and fold the corn chips carefully
and place them next to our cooler so
they will come home with us. They are
my favorites.

The next day i go to the kitchen for corn chips but
they are nowhere to be found; i look
everywhere and then
i go in the laundry room where she is
doing the wash and i ask her, Where
are the corn chips?
I left them there, to be nice,
she says and that is how the fight starts.
It goes on and on, but it ends the way
they always end: she is in tears and when

i try to comfort her by saying i love her, she
says, You don't love me; you don't
know what love is. And i am thinking,
not out loud of course, That's a
goddamn lie, i love
those corn chips.

Among the Rhetoricians

I do not mean these people any disrespect.
They are decent, hardworking school teachers
who have read too much and it has wrecked
their love of language like those poor preachers

on TV destroyed by too much religion.
Once when I was a boy, I got a BB gun;
I took it out and shot at a pigeon,
thinking that would be great fun

but to my horror, I hit and killed
it and then I threw the gun away.
The rhetoricians don't get that; so thrilled
by the mind's obsessive analytical play

they do not see that they kill the word:
they admire the gun and do not mourn the bird.

Lacks Punch

i knew him when he was just starting out,
a hot young poet looking to score and
mad as hell at all the self styled critics
and the big shot editors who sat in judgement

of the poems like little frog gods
sitting on a Lily saying who will live
on the page and who must die.
Oh how he hated those bastards but

now he edits a little mag of his own
and he asks me for some poems so
i send them and he sends them back.
The one about you not belonging and

the one about your mother's death
lack punch, he writes me and
i thought that was very good.
All old fighters finally lose their punch

and most stay on too long after it's gone,
hoping to get lucky one more time.
The only thing worse than a fighter
with no punch

is a man with a computer
and a mailing list who
thinks that makes him
a critic.

The Best Who Ever Lived

The young poet is sitting on the floor in front of me.
She is excited.
She has brought me her newest batch of poems and
she is on fire with it, it is eating her heart out
on its way to her Soul.
She wants to be the best, she
talks about what it takes to be the best,
what it would mean to be the best who ever lived.

I do not tell her that the cost is
more than any sane person would ever pay but
once you have the sickness you will pay
and gladly,
you will sell your heart and when that is
not enough to pay the rent on fame then
you will happily fork over your Soul;

i do not tell her about Memphis Johnny
who swept the floors in the factory where i worked.
Memphis Johnny had no teeth and bad skin and breath
but when he was a young man he made his name
as a sideshow geek in the carnivals.
Every cheap tawdry carnival used to have one,
a man, they were always men, who drew a crowd

by biting the heads off of live chickens,
eating live mice and worms and light bulbs and
crawling snakes and razor blades and lizards.
Everyone who ever saw Memphis Johnny
do his work said
he was the best who ever lived.

In the Ivy League

i knew i was out of my minor league
long before i ever set foot in Princeton, but
it was never clearer to me than one day when
i ran into the famous poet i shared an office with,
one day he would be the president

of one of the national poetry academies.
i had just gotten my copy of one of the little mags
where 5-6 of my poems were next to several
of Bukowski's and i said to the famous poet,
holding out the magazine to him, Have you seen

the latest issue of so-and-so? There's 3 poems
by Bukowski that will knock your socks off.
He looked down at the magazine and then up at me
with the kind of look you would give someone who
had used your guest towel to wipe his ass.

Bukowski? He sneered.
No wonder nobody ever sends their work
to that magazine, he said and that
was the only time me and the famous poet
ever spoke to one another.

Eating Lunch With the Nobel Laureate

Every so often while i was at Princeton,
the Writing faculty would gather for lunch.
One time i found myself next to the Nobel Laureate
who was holding forth on what a bad book
Huckleberry Finn was.

i like Huckleberry Finn, it's good, i volunteered.
She stopped dead in her tracks, mid-
sentence and stared at me.
In the end Huck has a failure of nerve;
he falls prey to the mind of the culture and Jim

becomes sub-human, a toy for Huck's amusement;
Huck betrays love, the original and only human sin
and Twain rubs our faces in it, i said to her.
She had a forkful of chocolate mousse halfway
to her mouth;

it fulfilled its destiny and then
she turned to face me.
I'm a writer and I know; trust me, she
said, Huckleberry Finn is a bad book.
She turned away to find intelligent conversation.

i ate the pasta and salad, passed
on the chocolate mousse though others
raved about how good it was.
Figures; what's an idiot like me
know about good?

Every Girl in Town Gets A Prize

We live in an age where a woman's beauty has
been so degraded that it now depends upon
the surgeon's knife and
the heart has lost its measure.
In this age, no one dares to offend
by having a strong opinion or making a claim
to the superiority of one thing over another. Thus
it came as no surprise when the local newspaper
announced that the traditional
Miss Drew County Beauty Pageant,
part of the annual Drew County Fair and
Livestock Exposition—the pageant theoretically

being part of the Fair, not the Livestock Exposition—
has been replaced with 9 different pageants,
ranging from Miss Drew County Pageant, open
to women ages 16-21, all the way through
Jr. Miss, Petite Miss, Pixey Miss and Tiny Tots pageants
to Drew Co. Baby Pageant, ages 0-23 months.

In each pageant there are 4 winners, including
Miss Congeniality, which goes to the young woman
who is most able to endure humiliation and torture
and never stop smiling. What i wonder is, why
they have deliberately ignored the unborn,
ages conception-birth.
Pregnant women should be x-rayed,
sonograms taken, a winner declared
Drew Co. Miss Zygote, get her

started on the path to womanhood
right away before she finds out
there is a fight to be fought here and
beauty is a thing you must pay for
with your life.

The Black Reward for A Roaring Life
(Dylan)

I cannot handle even the small power of the classroom
without an inner cruelty and tyranny arising,
married to a brazen arrogance, a blatant
showing off and always a smoldering rage.

My self importance roars like a Lion in a cage,
and like a rotting corpse I am trapped in the tomb
of habits. Keep power from me lest latent
monsters sleeping in their graves come terrorizing

the villagers in their homes. Power is my doom
and my torment; it strips me of my patient
facade and parades my shame naked upon the stage
for all to see. Shame is the black reward for compromising

honor with a cruel and petulant display;
small powers lead small men fast astray.

You Talk Too Much

I call the old woman every now and then.
She is unpleasant, coarse, her life is hell, she
finds fault with everything and then
she covers it quickly with a smile
and a denial but
when I was a small boy
she was very good to me,
the only one who was, so
I owe her and I mean to pay her back
with what little kindness I am capable of,
by taking it
and taking it from her
and not hitting back.
So I call her
and I am on the phone 2 minutes
trying to be pleasant when
she says,
You talk too much.
I look around me: there are
piles of dirty towels, one wet
in the sink, old socks by the door,
lint balls the size of Manhattan
under my bed, roaches bigger
than the lint balls on the walls,
the roof leaks, the faucets leak, the camper leaks,
my back is ruined so I cannot do hard work,
I haven't had sex in 2 years, no matter
how hard I shake it the pee still drips
down my leg, the muffler's broken, the

bunkhouse toilet is broken, the VCR
is broken. Yeah,
I say to her,
You're right.
That's what's wrong with me,
I talk too much.

Just Lucky, i Guess

i lost a dollar at the track today.
i went with $6, put 5 on the daily double
and won.
It paid $300 and now i was feeling lucky so
i let it all ride on a 30-1 shot in the 3rd and
he ran wire to wire. Now
i knew i was in the quiet zone
where the gods that view us with amusement
had infused me with grace.
i let it all ride, picking the favorite
in the 4th who won by 2 lengths and paid
3 for 2. i couldn't lose and i
knew it, i could feel the grace descending
like a ray of Sunlight in a dark hole
so i bet the whole stack, every penny of it
on this old jockey who had once been
one of the great and famous but women and drink
had brought him crashing down. This
was his first race back after a long time
drying out and cleaning up. That morning i thought
that i would bet on him because
he had paid something for his art and now
he was a sure thing waiting to happen.
He was on an ordinary horse in a race for 3 year olds
who had not won a stakes race, a perfect situation
for a wise and hungry has-been to make a comeback.
He would have been the sentimental favorite but
there is no sentiment at the track so at 8-1
i bet the whole stack.

Coming down the stretch he led by a nose and
then he made 2 brilliant moves:
along the rail was an opening with a horse
charging hard for it so without looking back
Jorge veers slightly—just enough so there
would not be an interference call—and he
closes off the hole, making the horse go wide;
then without a glance
he veers again to his right, making it seem
normal and without guile and
the speed horse can't get by him before the wire.
He wins by a nose and now
i have more money than i have ever seen,
over $100,000 and it is at that very moment,
when i begin to calculate how
one more win and i will be set for life, that
the laughing gods depart for other amusements
leaving me alone in hell,
but i am not quick enough to sense that they
have left me standing in my usual loser's shoes.
They leave me with just enough sense to pull out
$5 just in case
and i bet the whole stack in a very careful
and reasonable maneuver to place,
on the favorite who has won 3 stakes races in a row
and can't miss but he
does,
stumbling out of the gate, getting boxed
on the rail by Jorge of all people, the dirty

bastard he should have been called
for interference, and
finishing a distant 4th; Jorge wins on the
long shot, not even a protest.
i look around me, suddenly mortal again
and no one even notices that my life has collapsed
like a cheap trailer in a high wind.
i join the other losers at the bar, lay down
5 bucks and get 2 beers.
How'd you do, the bartender asks.
Lost a buck, i tell him.
Lucky, he says.

The Righteous Pimps and Whores

The little man and his little woman friend
talk about standing up for the truth, waiting
like jackals at the edge of a herd
for the old, the sick and the weak
to fall so they can
move in for the kill.

He boasts about the time he went after
the woman who advertised a catholic mass
in the student newspaper, a clear violation
of the separation of church and state,
he trumpets in his rightness, while she

boasts about the time she went after
a man who put his hand on her shoulder,
wrote him up for sexual harassment, sent
the letter to his boss.
They parade their truth until
i hate the truth
and must go out for fresh air or die
from the stink of righteousness.

The world is full of people sick with truth,
men lashing the naked buttocks of their young,
women nagging their loves to slow death,
the critics, the pimps, the hustlers, the whores
all killing for the truth
and i love the truth but in their hands

it is like a good dog who has
gotten a taste for blood and cannot stop
killing the chickens so
you have to take it out behind the barn,
a lump in your throat, and
put a bullet in its head.

College Boy

The worst job i ever had was at Steelcase in Grand Rapids
where i worked the assembly line making desk drawers
with mostly old men bitter in their days
after years of working a crummy job in a place

that used them up like cheap screws and then
threw them away and they all knew
what was in it for them at the end of the line.
i was a college boy there for the summer

and they didn't like college boys much, short-timers
they called them like in prison or the combat Marines.
They gave me shit and shit jobs: every mistake
the inspectors caught, they made me do the repairs,

no piece-work, just the low hourly rate to iron out
their dings and dents, their weak welds and loose handles.
but once on our break one of them called me college boy
one time too often and because i was weak and

full of self-importance i turned on him in a rage.
You'll be here until you die, i shot back hard at him,
but I'll get a degree and be your boss and
fire your ass some day, i said and

no one spoke. They all looked away because
all of us knew it was the truth,
but it was a hard, mean truth and
not one worth saying;

it was the kind of thing that
gives the truth a bad name.

And They Say A Man Can't Change

One of my former students is visiting me and he
is looking over my current course outline when
he sees it: Hey, he says, you've changed it so

a rewrite's worth 5 points now and
the rewrite's optional, how come?
So I tell him about Bo who was as big

as 2 brick houses stacked on top of each other
and as mean as a pit bull with a tick
on his dick.

One day he comes out of class in a bad mood
and I start ragging him about his rewrite and
the 2 points it will cost him not to do it

and he takes it for about as long as I can go
on one breath and then he says,
You shut your goddamn piehole

before I beat your sorry ass. Well
that right there would have been enough
for any sane man but

I trail along behind him yapping like
a starving mongrel nipping at the heels of
a Brahma Bull and then he

throws his books down all over the floor,

turns on me and says, Sumbitch,
are you ready to die for them 2 points? And

that right there is when I decided
to make it 5 points and
make the rewrite optional.

As Alone As It Ever Gets

It is late when i round the curve near the grade school
and there frozen in my headlights
a hit deer is sitting in the road,
unable to move, gazing straight into me,

piercing the careful manufactured distance
between us and the natural world.
It all comes crashing down in the artificial light
and like numbers flashing on a tote board

my choices slam past me: if i stop, what
exactly will i do, drag it by the legs
off to the side of the road; will it even
let me get near it; will i hurt it more

if i do; will someone hit it coming too fast
around that curve and kill it; will that
be a mercy?
It is sitting there, its beautiful head up and

as the last hot question ratchets into its slot
i have swerved past it and my only concern is
that the car coming towards me will think i did it.
You can go for years, nothing happening,

and then in a single moment
you are revealed in a merciless light
for just exactly what you are and
how far you have traveled to get there.

When the Laughter Died

When I was a small child
my father loved to tell me jokes after
dinner and I loved to laugh at them, wild
silly jokes, uncontrollable laughter

out loud at the dining room table;
it was our way of showing what we felt inside.
Then his beatings grew worse and soon he was unable
to make me smile; finally the laughter died.

Once the laughter died in childhood
it never mattered
what was left; like a fine china cup it was shattered
and no good:

you can glue it with the greatest delicacy
but it still won't hold any tea.

The King of the Losers

A place where losers like my Father went
to drink when they didn't even have money for the rent
was a dive called Stinky Reed's River Inn;
the drinks were cheap there but thin

because Stinky watered the liquor. It was plain
and everyone knew it, but nobody complained
because he often gave it away and he charged half the price
of any place else in town. He was basically a nice

crook, a smiling cheat. It's smart for a thief
to smile and set up free drinks; in their ordinary grief
people are stupid. Stinky was chief among the losers,
smiling as he slapped backs and cheated the dying boozers.

The last rat on a sinking ship will often smile
because at least he gets to be captain for awhile.

No Sanctuary

Sometimes at night after he was drunk and asleep in his chair,
I crept frightened down the silent darkened stair

to be near my snoring boozed up father so my dreams
did not scare me, wondering if I could waken him with screams

before the imagined murderers huddled on our porch, who would
murder him and rape my mother and sister, could

break through the door. Sometimes as he sat there,
sprawled and senseless in his underwear,

I held his foot, trying to make him human, afraid my touch
would waken him, praying he would love me half as much

as I loved him. Hungry for the touch he could not give
I huddled in the dark and wondered if we'd live;

in their teeming brains, whatever frail reason children spin
cannot conceive that the gravest danger lies within.

Everything They Told Us Was Wrong

When i was a boy i had a big picture book of Elephants
which i looked at almost every day;
i loved the Elephants.
Knowing there were Elephants on the Earth
made it easier for me to be here, despite the fact
that everywhere i looked, human wreckage
littered the landscape, starting with
my Mother and Father, broken and ruined
by drink.
Then one day they took me to Chicago's Lincoln Park Zoo.

I was excited because everyone else was excited and
i would get to see the Elephants.
What i saw broke my heart.
It was the cages.

They tried to explain to me about the cages
but i knew it was lies, because
i saw the Elephants.
One of them lay there staring and
she never moved.
Next to her a large bull Elephant in his cage
paced without ceasing, back
and forth, back and forth.
It was agony and i began to cry.

They could not console me, though they tried
and soon we had to leave, everyone
angry and yelling at me and

when we got home my Father spanked me.

I was 8 years old and
that was when i understood
that i was trapped and
if they could do that to the Elephants
and lie about it, then
they were capable of
anything.

Astaire & Rogers & Citation

My Father was a brutal, hopeless, incurable drunk
but just as Astaire needed Rogers,
my Father needed my Mother, who
was thrilled to play his lovely victim.
She had all the moves:
her timing was impeccable,
she loved to play to a packed house,
her method was the whine and the complaint,
she was a world-class nag and
it drove him to magnificent heights of cruelty,
physical, mental, emotional, a performer
of great depth and enormous range.

Together, they starred in all the bars
in central Illinois but they saved their finest performances
for Ben's Barn where we ate every Saturday night
of my childhood, one of the longest
continuous runs in the profession.
There my Father and Mother were at the top of their form,
the Fred and Ginger of the drunk set,
he pinching waitresses' butts,
she weeping and yelling in her shrillest soprano:
You don't ever have sex with me anymore, all you
care about is waitresses and hotel whores;
she matched every slick move he made
only backwards, until

everyone in the Barn was turned in their stalls,
yes they had booth-stalls with the names

of famous winners of the Kentucky Derby on them.
We always shared a stall with Citation, and
once all the eyes were on her, my Mother
stumbled to her feet whining and sobbing and
he shoved her hard back into the booth
where she hit her head or bruised her shin or
turned her ankle or skinned her elbow, the waitress
of pinched butt brought a wet towel and

they exited in grand style, him
bruising her arm with rough handling, she
screeching that he was breaking her arm, me
and my sister trailing along to great critical sympathy
in supporting roles, chorus dancers.
Astaire was not as great without Rogers and
when my Mother came dancing
down the home stretch, no nag alive
could beat her in her prime;
with her in the race,
Citation never even got out of his stall.

The House I Grew Up In

It was a beautiful house from the outside,
2 stories, screened porch looking out over the backyard,
the last house on a dead-end road, beyond it
a woods that stretched for miles, trees, creek,
owls, snaked, the works, paradise even, except

for the corruption within.
Hell looked lovely from the outside, but drink
sickened everything it touched starting with my parents,
but without mercy on my sister and i as well.
The beatings, the screaming hair-pulling fist fights

of my Mother and Father had the neighbors
up and down the street lined up in the drive next door
watching until one couldn't take it anymore and,
afraid for the children, who were upstairs looking out
at them ashamed, called the police and then

2 squads in the driveway, red lights flashing, notebooks
out taking it all down from the neighbors, one
armed uniformed giant always climbing the stairs
to check on us, i guess to see if we had lived.
That house still stands. The Romans had it right:

when a place was sacked and drenched with gore,
they burned and razed the town, leveled it and then
they salted the Earth so that
nothing would grow there for 100s of years and
no one would ever think of living there again.

At My Mother's Funeral

Understand, i am not complaining, this
is not a complaint, it is a lament.
She died; with that i have no argument.
With her ruined drunken life, death was bliss;

she was a dreadful mother, killed by wine,
unable to deal with her crippling dread
of life, married to a mean drunk who bled
what good was in her dry. She did not shine

but she was my Mother and who will care
that for her funeral, 5 people showed up.
She drank to stop time; it never slowed up;
damn the world for ignoring her, how dare

it? When your mother dies, cities should burn
and the slow galaxies should cease to turn.

The Plumber

It is freezing cold and our toilet hasn't worked
in 4 goddamn days; we pee out the backdoor and it
freezes before it hits the ground so we
call the plumber, then another and another.
They are all too busy, so out of desperation
i call the one guy everyone says to avoid.
He's a crook, he'll rip you off,
they all say but
he is the only one who will come so
i tell him to come on out.
There are 2 of them in the truck,
the big fat mean one with the mustache
and the skinny bent old man who
does all the dirty work and agrees
with everything the fat boy says.
i call the fat boy aside.
Snot is frozen in his mustache.
The quote you gave me is way too high, i say;
Roger Miller did this job 6 months ago and he
charged us $30 less.
Why isn't he here doing it now, he says?
Couldn't come.
How many others did you call?
2.
Where are they?
Couldn't come.
That's why you're paying me, he says and then
he gets this nasty look on his face and leans in
real close and says,

Every minute you waste bullshitting me
the cost goes up. Now,
do you want us to do the job or not?
Yep, i say swallowing it hard but
choking it down. What you find out when
the shit won't flush away and
you have to shit in the freezing rain is
exactly how much shit
you are willing to eat.

Wasichu

The Lakota Sioux
called the white man Wasichu
which means, The-One-Who-Steals-the-Fat.
The Lakota were subsistence hunters, and that

life was built on trust. The hunter who killed game
was rewarded with fat for his family. In this same
way everyone got a portion, fat being a must
in their meager diet. Above all, the Lakota were a just

people. In every tribe the worst criminal was he who
stole fat from his fellows; they tore the clothes off the wasichu
and beat him with sticks, driving him away.
One who stole fat from the common store could not stay

among the people for he lacked the compassionate feeling
which breaks the heart to think of such stealing.

The Measure of the Human Condition

We are in the process of reducing the world
to us, and yet
there is no discernible reduction
in our urge to kill, so

we are left with killing ourselves.
One measure of our inner state is that
we are in the very midst of the
6th great extinction, an ecological disaster

unseen on this planet in 50 million years,
since the eradication of the dinosaurs.
It has been argued that
that purge was nature's way of eliminating

an evolutionary error, a creature
who had grown too big for its own good.
The argument goes that there are
important lessons to be learned from that event but

what reveals most about the human condition is that
the current extinction event is almost exclusively
due to the behavior of mankind and in the very midst of
a planetary catastrophe of Biblical proportions,

only a handful of humans even notice it.

Running On Empty

i am in this town in southern California,
a lovely little town somewhere in the desert
where everything is green and blooming,
every yard has beautiful flowers and
exotic trees, the green lawns are manicured.
The first morning i go for a walk

and that's when i notice it.
Everywhere i walk, i see that beneath the grass
there is no dirt, it is
all sand, just sand and
every morning and every evening
all over town there is a little click followed by

the hissing as the automatic sprinklers come on.
And late at night when they are dreaming,
the street sweepers move in all over town,
sweeping the sand back out of the streets,
keeping the desert at bay. On the edge of town
there is a land-sale sign: $4,000 an acre, and

i think to myself, My God, people pay $4,000
for desert sand. There is no end to it, no limit
upon the madness of humans, they will buy anything,
build entire towns on desert sand where the water
is in short supply and will soon run out because
they and millions like them are sucking the Colorado River

bone dry.

The sprinklers come on and they suck the water
to feed the fever dreams.
The madhouses are full of people with ideas
no crazier than this. Some get lucky and
for them the desert blooms,

others not, and they wind up in padded rooms.

Driving Through Logging Country On the Way to White Rock Mountain

The logging trucks are dinosaurs,
their huge weight crushing the Earth,
their blank eyes blazing at night,
and cold in the noonday Sun;
their rumbling roar rolling through the hills
can be heard for miles, they are

omnivores consuming entire forests,
always hungry, never satisfied.
A sharp turn in the winding road
and we come upon vast stretches
which they have devoured,
nothing moving, no shade,

the stunned stupid silence stretching
like the eyes of a hurt animal
all the way to the sawmill town.
In the little town the women
are plain, lean and muscular;
they have no more dreams.

The men are in blue overalls and
they do not believe in love.
If you speak to them the young men
defer to the older ones,
decent men trying to stay alive
in a hard place where the only wealth

was the hardwood, the old growth
Oak, Sycamore, Hickory, Ash,
Cedar, Elm, Birch, Maple.
They cut because we demand it but
they pay a price for
taking down the old grandfather trees,

we can see it in their eyes:
they are hard, sad and lonely;
they have no more shade, no more shelter
from the Sun; the birds
do not sing here and the animals
no longer come around;

they are dying
from a great loneliness of the spirit.
When Fall comes, there is no color left
on the mountainside and nothing falls
except the last tree placed upon the last truck
heading for the next town.

The wind does not rustle, it blows cold and hard;
no Lark awakens them to morning, no
Owl settles them to night; the silence
between them is not softened by the lost leaf
casting no more shadow upon the face;
they are left to go on in what remains

of their lives, the dream
having once more failed them.

Red Hawk Is Not An Indian Name

The great disease of the human spirit is possession.
We believe we can own everything: our children,
our lovers, our lives, the Earth.
The fact is that we own almost nothing but

The Earth owns us. That does not stop us
from making absurd claims.
The Indians once understood the trap of ownership,
but now are not exempt from the common madness.

Some of them make a big deal of my name,
saying it is an Indian name so
i have no right to it;
it is not an Indian name, it is an Earth name,

it belongs to the Earth.
One time i was invited to a Sweat Lodge ceremony
with some young Indians who thought the Sweat Lodge
belonged to them. They had all done prison time and

believed they were real bad asses
so they decided to turn up the heat in the Lodge
and smoke out the white boy.
They turned it up all the way and pretty soon

they were falling out of the Lodge, until
all who remained were the man pouring the water
and me; we sat there and cooked.
You can't fool the Sweat Lodge.

It reveals everything, courage and stupidity
alike. Courage comes from the Earth;
stupidity is the only thing
we can honestly claim as our own.

Conscious Suffering is Sacrificial Bodily Prayer

We are taught superficial prayer only, with mouth and words
but very few of us, except in the dark-skinned
churches of ecstatic worship, ever pray with our bodies, like birds
sailing upon a current of air, or scaled and finned

creatures riding a wave: this is bodily prayer
of one kind. Another is conscious suffering, the circumstance
whereby a human voluntarily takes on the pain of her Creator
bodily, such as the native tribal prayer of the Sun Dance

where the body is pierced and stretched upon leather thongs,
released only when the skin tears or the dancer passes out from
    exhaustion;
this form of prayer asks nothing of God, but takes all of the wrongs
of humanity upon the body as suffering, a form of crucifixion,

just as a woman enters into the broken prayer of childbirth
and delivers redemption for the suffering we have brought upon the
    Earth.

Brat on Rye With Onions

Willie takes me to Tom's 12th Street Barbecue.
Best BBQ in the country, he says and when we walk in
i am overwhelmed with the smell of the meat,
pork, beef and chicken, sauce mild or hot,
onions and peppers mild or hot, home made
onion buns or rye bread, it is
all nude nostril ecstacy on an onion bun.

The waitress has big tits and slattern eyes and
she leans way over me to place my utensils, her
heavy breasts dangling and brushing my shoulder.
What'll it be boys, she says and with those big red
bruised lips of hers i can only think of sausage so
i am just about to order when
it all comes back to me like a mescaline vision:

once when i was a Boy Scout we went on a field trip
to the Union Stockyards on the south side of Chicago and
they led us in to see the pigs being slaughtered.
The smell was so strong it made me gag but i watched
a vision of hell unfolding there that i never forgot;
the pigs came out a chute bawling and a big brawny
man in overalls grabbed one by its hind legs and with

one clean sweep hooked it in the groin with an iron hook
which jerked it off the floor screaming upside down and
2 men in goggles, surgical caps, rubber gloves to the elbows,
rubber boots to the knee, and rubber aprons, arms and chests bare,
stood waiting there for the line of screaming pigs.

The first man hit the lead pig one time in the head with a stun gun,
the next one on the other side stood there with a long sharp knife

and he sliced the pig's throat with one stroke;
blood shot 8-10 feet, they were covered in blood and
then the pig disappeared through long rubber strips,
the overhead line carrying it to the next circle of hell but
the Boy Scouts had seen enough; we backed out of there
quiet for the first time on the trip and 3 of us
threw up; we did not eat hot dogs for a week.

Brat on rye with onions, i say and her
bosom heaves as if i have asked her to marry me.
As she walks away her buttocks roll beneath her
skin tight uniform like 2 pigs in a burlap sack.
Waitresses are screaming their orders over the din,
customers lined up along the wall waiting for tables.
The onions are fried in grease and they are sweet and good.

She licks her lips as she gives us the check and
we leave her a great big fat juicy tip.

Good Vibrations

Ark City, Kansas got this slaughterhouse
which kills 2,000 beef cattle a day, 6 days
a week, i think they don't slaughter on Sundays,
Christian you know and

this saved the town's economy.
What gets me is the vibrations.
Everyone these days knows about vibes, even
straight people, even the good people of

Ark City know about vibes, how a mean dog
or a dangerous man or a whore all
put out these vibes that can really
have an effect on a person's mental and

emotional state and
right here in their midst, 6 days a week,
2,000 large living creatures are being slaughtered.
They raise their children in that, they

pray and grill their steaks in that and still
they are oblivious to the fact that in us
is a thing which hungers and can never be filled
by all the meat in the world and

this thing which hungers can be ruined
by crude or subtle means, by
direct actions or the vibrations which ensue,
by the butcher's knife or

what remains when it is laid aside.

The United States Senate

On TV just now they are interviewing the latest
U.S. Senator to get caught in a scandal. This one
is married with 3 kids and shacked up with a
Senate intern barely out of her teens. That
wasn't so bad, hell all of them sleep with
young women, but this woman disappeared.

No trace, no corpse, no clues, just
dropped out of sight and was
never seen again.
i listen for a moment to his lies, wondering
at the corruption of the U.S. Senate, how
lies and treachery and betrayal are

so ingrained in its history, lie after lie
to the Indians to steal the land,
treachery to the slaves before emancipation,
betrayal after for 100 years. Then
i switch channels and the first thing i come to
is professional wrestling,

the most blatantly dishonest, lying
in-your-face con on television.
i sit back
and relax,
feeling cleaner
already.

The Hungry Ghost

The president is on TV just now waving the flag,
explaining how we must be brave and send our young boys
to die
in order to protect this flag, and he
points to it, there on the wall
a big red white and blue flag.
He's got a tiny one pinned to his lapel

and in the audience hundreds of people cheer
and wave little cloth flags back at him.
Oh my, after 10,000 years of this, after
generation upon generation upon generation
of young boys marching to their deaths, how
can we not know that the flags are always changing
with the arbitrary lines they draw on a map?

After 10,000 years of bloody death,
after 100 million dead in the twentieth century,
the bloodiest century in the history of mankind,
how can we not yet see that standing behind every flag
is the Hungry Ghost
starving for our juicy emotions, our fear and hatred,
mouth watering for the next course of young boys and

we wave the flag, we
cheer and scream and weep and pull our hair and
we send them rank and file by the millions
marching straight into the oven to be roasted
while the Hungry Ghost stands by exhorting us,

in one hand a sharpened boning knife,
in the other

a flag.

The End of the World and Burning In Hell Forever

What i am talking about is the True Believer,
the chapter and verse, there's only one way
to heaven and that's my way, finger
in your face, if you aren't saved you will
burn in hell forever, True Believer.

i have them in my classes all the time.
At semester's end on their evaluations
they will say, This is the best class i have
ever had, but there's just one thing that
really bugs me and it is that you are

not saved; I'm begging you to accept Jesus
as your Lord and Savior or you will go to hell.
Other than that, I loved everything
about your class.
They talk about the end of the world the way

most people talk about crossing the street.
Why didn't you do your homework?
Doesn't matter, the world's going to end.
Why weren't you in class yesterday?
The rapture's coming.

What i wonder is why you never see any of them
laughing and having a good time, joking around
and taking it easy. Of course, if the world
really does end and we all burn in hell forever,
i guess the joke is on us.

The President is Just Another Sexually Repressed Male Terrorist

On TV, he stands before us flanked by servile senators,
those obsequious dogs, and explains why we must go to war
against yet another tiny country who has no chance.
In a century of unspeakable evils like the 20th, perhaps

the worst evil is the systematic sexual repression of males
by our society. It has produced the unspeakable evil;
the universal creative force must flow unimpeded like a river
because where it is dammed it becomes a poison which

turns in upon itself and destroys all that is good.
It poisons the Earth and everything on it, it produces
monstrous weapons of terrifying destruction, men hit and rape
and hurt their women and children, and fear follows them

like a fawning dog follows a tyrant.
In the shadow of the sexual repression of males
stands a universal terrorism such that no sane woman
would willingly walk alone and unafraid after dark in any major city

in this country and they all teach their children
at the earliest possible opportunity about the dangers
of strange men in cars or on foot offering candy, but
they stand cowed and helpless before the terrorists who

sleep in their own beds and
enter their nurseries at will.
Our foreign policy, our education system, our religion,
our media, our diet, our entertainment, the very

structure of our civilization is grounded in
the systematic repression of male sexual energy;
it has created a billion dollar pornography industry,
the dehumanization of the female body to sell

every conceivable item from beer to cars, and the cruel
insanity which drives desperate women to surgically alter
every part of their bodies in order to satisfy
the insatiable longing of repressed male sexuality.

Women and children live with male terrorists
and are, of course, terrified to such an extent that
they do not even see it; it is so woven into the very fabric
of their language and lives that it has become nearly invisible.

Men are so terrified
of sexual intimacy that they would rather
hurt women by turning upon them or away from them,
than bow down before them in worship and adoration,

bathing their feet in tears of gratitude and
drying them with their hair. Men are so terrified
they would rather hit their children than hold them
and shower them with devotion all of their lives.

The president finishes and
the senators stand as one body to applaud him.
In half-a-million homes, young men rise
and prepare to go to their deaths.

The Way Things Are

Nature always gets what it needs.
It cultivates humans and then it feeds
on our release of negative emotions; it breeds
us the way a man breeds a herd of sheep
and we do not mind the slaughter because we are asleep,
dead and oblivious to the reality of the world, deep

in our unconscious driven desire
while within we are burned alive by the fire
of our wanting. We are pacified by what we aspire
to: money, sex, power, drugs, god, fame,
it all has the same
intent, it keeps us passive and tame

until the sheep are fattened; they are doomed,
sheared, slaughtered, boned, quartered and consumed.

Part ii. The Seeker: the middle world
("Seek and ye shall find." Jesus)

"Seeker!
Empty the boat,
Lighten the load,
Passion and desire and hatred...

Are you quiet?
Quieten your body.
Quieten your mind...

By your own efforts
Waken yourself, watch yourself.
And live joyfully...

Life is easy
For the man who is without shame,
Impudent as a crow,
A vicious gossip,
Vain, meddlesome, dissolute.

But life is hard
For the man who quietly undertakes
The way of perfection,
With purity, detachment and vigor...

How easy it is to see your brother's faults,
How hard to face your own.
You winnow his in the wind like chaff,
But yours you hide,
Like a cheat covering up an unlucky throw."

– Buddha, *The Dhammapada*, 96–97, 143–144, 146.

Easier To See A Mote in Your Neighbor's Eye

A gifted spiritual Teacher asks
if i will perform a simple task
with His people in Little Rock.

i think i did a fine job, so it's a shock
when i get a stern rebuke from my Master
who tells me what i did was a disaster,
no matter how many were helped, how many renewed,
because i did it with the wrong attitude:

the operation was a success, i reported with pride,
overlooking the fact that the patient died;
i helped them to see their Attention was weak,
but was arrogant when i needed to be gentle and meek;
the right thing done for the wrong reason,
is doomed like the rose which blooms out of season.

The Unspeakable Loneliness of Being

Grandma and Aunt Mary had an old cat named Bones
and when they found that tumors on its spine
were the cause of its convulsions, those 2 shriveled crones
made me kill it. How, i said. They gave me a shovel. I was 9.

I didn't want to do it, cried as i carried Bones in one hand,
the shovel in the other. I hit him as hard as i could,
right between the eyes. To my horror he convulsed and tried to stand,
his bloody head an awful sight. I knew then i'd never be good

after doing a thing like this. A Crow from Hades lit in the tree
waiting on me to finish Bones off. All the God went out of the world
with the second blow, and all the joy out of me.
On my knees i dug a hole for the curled

up lifeless Bones and ceased forever being young;
in that broken breath i learned the unspeakable human tongue.

What Happens When A Lawyer is Made to Pay

Jeanne Louise Calment was a French woman
who was born in 1875 and
lived in Paris when fine apartments were at a premium,
extremely hard to come by
except by luck or guile.

She had a smart lawyer who
coveted her elegant apartment
and kept after her to assign it to him
upon her death.
By 1965 she had had enough;

90 years old, she agreed,
making a deal with him that
he would pay her a handsome monthly stipend
until her death when
he would take ownership of the apartment.

But she fooled him.
She lived for another 32 years,
the oldest person known to French science and
her lawyer's payments far exceeded
the value of her apartment.

She outlived the fool by 2 years
and when he died they
shut down hell for a day
and rejoiced in the streets
to welcome him.

They give the citizens of hell a day off
only when its streets ice over or
when a lawyer
is outsmarted and
made to pay.

Hurt Dog By the Road

Brian and I are driving
through a hard snow, 10 below
trying to get home
when through the blinding flakes

just at the edge of our headlights
we see something struggling,
clawing at the side of the road.
We stop. It's a badly hurt dog

someone has hit in the blizzard,
maybe didn't even know it.
We come close and it looks up
with those terribly wounded eyes.

Something in the eyes of hurt animals
is so close to God that we
cannot bear to look for long
before we have to turn away.

I do not know what to do but
Brian is a hunter, he
gets his rifle from the truck.
Oh no, I say, Can't we....

You gonna take it to your house,
you gonna doctor it, feed it,
nurse it and watch it die slow,
he says and right there

it is all on me, all
the nice ideas about what I am
and what it means to be good
stare up at me

through the snow and
I am shaking but
not from the cold.
Go 'head, I say

and then I kneel down and
put one hand on the dog's broken back
softly because
it is the only gesture I can make

so that our lives count for something
as the shot rings out and we
cover it with snow,
drive the rest of the way

without speaking.
Sometimes the world stops for a moment
and a window opens into the Heart of Life,
no noise of thought,

where things suffer and die
without meaning or
the niceties of faith.
Then we see how little we are

and how vast the tapestry,
how cruel and beautiful
is the Heart of God beating in
such strange and far-away creatures

as ourselves.

Men

I wonder about us, how we are trained to fight wars,
to be brutal in our feelings if we feel at all
and treat good and decent women like night whores.
I have seen what happens when men reel and fall

into the savagery of war, how once they are broken
by the horror, they kill and loot and rape.
I wonder how a man can hold a woman down, no word spoken
as he covers her mouth and his friends line up, drape

their bodies across the frozen flesh, smother
her cries and look into her widened eyes, those dark pools
of sorrow and not think of his daughter, sister, mother
and stop, beg forgiveness, do whatever it is fools

must do to reclaim their humanity. When all hope is gone,
a Thing is born, comes from its cave alone
looking for anything, a fragile fawn,
something to hurt, in its hand a bone.

I have seen this Thing in me
hiding in its hole,
with its hand over its face so it cannot see
or be seen by the Soul.

What Is This Shit?

I am at a conference of writing teachers
where they read aloud the papers they wrote
and the writing is heartbreakingly bad,
it is no wonder the young hate writing
and I am thinking to myself,
What is this shit? when I remember

what my Guru said:
Be very very careful when judging
the works of others that you are
not too harsh because some day
someone will pick up your Soul
and they will read

what is written there and
if they read that you were kind, well
it may inspire them to be likewise but
if they do not find kindness,
those who read the Souls will give you
exactly what you deserve and

you do not want that,
do you? One of them who
said she admires my poetry finishes
reading her paper, comes up to me.
What do you think, she says,
be honest.

Nice, I say,

very nice.
Satisfied,
we both walk off
down our separate roads
to hell.

She Awakens to A Deeper Longing

She sat in the front row of my class,
tough and angry ever since she first found out
that the world was unkind.
She would not yield to tenderness
though sometimes against her will she smiled
and when she did her face lit up,
a thing of real beauty, her brown skin fair
and smooth with radiance, her brown eyes
cast shyly down as if she did not know
where such a sudden surge of joy came from,
only that it could not be trusted.

Then one day i called her to my office
to work out some minor offense i can barely remember
and when she told me her story, i believed her,
i saw she was no liar, though i could see
she did not expect to be believed, looked up at me,
then down, then up again and when i said to her,
i believe in you, she wept.
Not just a little, but for a long time,
all her toughness melting away like the last
remnant of snow in a Spring rain. In an unkind world,
kindness walks the thin line between life and death,

grieving all the way.

You May Think It Is Easy Being A Teacher

Everyone is going through a terrible struggle,
facing certain death,
trying to hold it all together, trying desperately
not to scream.

For 22 years George took it, rarely spoke,
kept to himself, taught in the Ed. Department.
Day after day he stood there before them
repeating it over and over and

over again and then one day,
you can look it up if you don't believe me but
I swear this is the way it happened, George
took off all his clothes,

stripped naked in front of his Elementary Ed. Class.
The girls cried out, made a horrified ruckus so
people came running from all over the building and
when they came through the door,

before they could grab him
George took off screaming down the hall,
naked,
things flopping and flying everywhere,

out the door and across campus, laughing
the kind of laugh you do not want to hear
twice and
people in wild chase of him, crowds

piling out of classrooms, some cheering and
laughing, some ashamed, some in sorrow because
they knew what it meant but
George gave all those girls in Elementary Ed.

something to think about that day, something
to consider about the cost of their profession.
You may think it is easy being a teacher but
when they caught up with George out on the highway

he just smiled quietly and they carried him off
and we never saw or heard from him again.
They have a place for those
who scream.

The Luck of the Draw

In my 40 years of writing the poems
i got lucky maybe half a dozen times,
you could say pitied by God who
must have tired of waiting on the rhymes

to come to me of my own accord
and bent down, half in sorrow, half in wrath
and thanks to the generosity of our Lord
there are 6 poems in 40 years that do not

add to the general garbage heap of mankind.
If getting lucky half a dozen times is your fate,
you will generally be known as one of the good poets;
a dozen times and you are great.

The fence that separates mediocre from great is flimsy,
composed entirely of God's whimsy.

A Known Entity on the Poetry Scene

The editor of one of the journals of dissent
writes me a whiney self-pitying letter telling
how some university threw him out because
he could not keep his mouth shut,
could not understand that sooner or later
because there's only so much in you,
you've got to save it for the poems

not waste it on the assholes who
never read a poem and do not care
if one more poet lives or dies.
He wants me to help him get a teaching job;
he wants one of my books and some poems
so I send them because I owe a debt to the poems
and this is one way I pay it off.

I never hear from him again but months later
a friend sends me the issue
my poems were supposed to be in.
No poems but in their place is a whiney,
self-pitying attack on me disguised as a
book review, like a whore
in a cheap wig.

Pissed because I ignored his job request,
he says I am a Known Entity on the poetry scene
and I must be criticized
for my name, my fame, and my poetry game.
That same month 2 young boys gun down

25 of their classmates and DiMaggio dies.
The voice of dissent is a precious thing

but in the hands of amateurs
many will die needlessly. On the other hand,
Joe hit in 56 straight games
and there is a small consolation,
a terrible beauty in that.
The Known Entity pours a cold one
and salutes the perfection of 56 straight;

in this vicious world where everyone
is a helpless burning thing
fighting a terrible lonely battle,
kindness
is the highest form of dissent,
after that
perfection of the craft.

The Land Has Teeth and It Knows the Truth

At the trailhead on White Rock Mountain, there is a sign
which warns of the sheer cliffs at the trail's edge,
no guard rails, then it lists the dead,
mostly young.
My name is not yet on that list; i am
no longer young though i do not assume that exempts me.

Just a little ways down the trail, maybe 200 yards,
there is a second sign warning what to do if you
meet a Bear on the trail.
If the first sign doesn't do it, the second one
stops all but the most determined or foolish hikers.
The second sign offers no solace for the aged,

it strips me of the veneer of civilization,
the illusion of security, places me squarely
into it: small mammal,
unarmed, fairly weak, moderately slow, prey,
meat,
lunch.

Standing there alone in the trees, leaves still dripping
from the rain, wet loam dirt smell heavy in the air,
no one is fooled; here is the plain truth:
the Earth owns us, we belong to the Earth;
we can rape, bomb and pillage, blame and justify, but
the Earth will not soon die, we will.

We must assume that something here tells the truth,
otherwise our lives, small and brutish as they are,
are utterly without meaning, and we can assume
that it is not humans who do so, history
is relentless on this point;
that leaves the land and the beasts of the land.

Just behind me there is a snap and a rustle of leaves.
i leap onto a boulder and turn, ready to face it;
a squirrel scampers across the trail, another in hot pursuit.
A laughter rises in me from the deep wellspring, not
from mind but from the Soul. i head on down the trail,
nothing left to lose.

Of all the suggestions on the Bear sign,
laughter is not one of them.

The Poetry Game

i have not had much luck at the game,
an occasional grant or fellowship,
a brief score at a big magazine
now and then

but mostly rejections, no tenure
at the first dump i taught in,
nice notes from the big time editors
urging me to send more poems

and the piles of poems keep on growing
while the stack of money dwindles
and then disappears.
Now i am a clerk at a bookstore,

50 years old and recommending nice
romance novels to no longer young women
who like myself have not had the luck.
But today this young woman comes in and

she is beautiful. Aren't you the poet,
she asks and when i admit it she smiles
and wants to buy my books. Then
she asks me who are the good poets

in the poetry section so i show her
the others and she buys both of them too.
She asks me to sign her copy
of my book and when i do she leans close

so her breasts are heavy against my arm
and her breath is sweet and warm
on my cheek. Maybe we'll see each other
at the readings downtown, she says to me

as she leaves and her smile makes the years
fall away like the promises of lovers.
Ahh, the poetry game, i think to myself
as i watch her tight jeans move off,

it has been good to me.

The Leper

One of the many hot-eyed young boys
has started up yet another little magazine.
He wants to publish the talent and
he can't stand those who have it.
Like so many young boys with matches
he wants to set fire to everything he sees
instead of conserving the matches
for the winter when
a good fire can save you.

He attacks all poets with teaching jobs.
I don't blame him, we're mainly hacks,
but he cuts us all with the same knife
as if we were all lepers
dragging our rotting carcasses outside
the walls of the city, bells
around our necks to warn the people
to stay away, and
generally they do.

He provides a most valuable service however;
one of the ways you know you've got it is
when those with no discernible talent
attack you viciously and other no-talents
agree.

He is right about one thing,
the university poetry is mostly rotten,
without fire or nerve of any kind,

poets hiding behind the poem.
There is very little competition
here on the outskirts of town;
bells ringing,
I keep on writing because
I am the leper
with the most fingers.

The Things That Most Reveal Us
(for Hayden & Mary Oliver)

You can tell a lot about a person's nature
by how they divide a hot apple pie.
Never mind their fame or social stature,
less is revealed by looking in their eye

than by observing them with knife in hand
before an apple pie. If they are miserly and greed
runs in their blood, 8 slices will stand
in silent witness to their unspoken need;

at a friend's house i was asked to cut the pie
but she told me to make enough for all 6
of us and i was forced to comply.
If numbers demand, you're in a real fix,

or if someone else is giving the orders,
but if it's up to me, i prefer quarters.

The Dancer Is the Dance

Fonteyn's simplest ballet poses gave such integrity to the line
of her elegant muscled form, her faultless beauty was so pure,
that she made the female body a moral force;
her presence was a natural Law whose source
was not human so she suffered when made to endure
human love, the coarse violating the fine.

Yet it was aging that brought forth her greatest gifts:
when she could no longer leap, she grew still,
waited for the music to envelop her, drowned
in a silence more majestic than the flying lifts
and younger pirouettes; pausing for her heart to fill,
she was motion with an inner calm, downed

Eagle stately in repose, life coiled in womb,
poised to explode. Only cancer made her Earth-bound,
crippled her foot so she dragged it behind her,
but she refused amputation; it was a constant reminder
that the fiercest leap must come to ground,
the finest beauty's ravished by the tomb.

A Game of No Chance

Listen, we could bullshit each other,
i know you are good at it and you know
i am better so let's play our cards
face up, with an open hand.
i'll show you what i've got,
you do the same, for once
we'll play it straight.

Okay, i am a third-rate pimp.
i sell myself on the avenue of broken dreams,
i lie down with the bums, the whores, the derelicts,
the losers who can't bear the sight of themselves
in the cracked glass mission windows.
i don't drink, i don't shoot dope or
smoke crack or sell it to those who do.
Nope, i am a pusher of the real hard stuff;
i sell self-hate and where i sit
everyone is buying because
they cannot resist hating themselves.
i sell myself and
i sell short, i sell cheap and
i sell out.
i am a pimp and i am the only whore
who will be seen with me, i sell
diseased, wasted, broken dreams
and i am my best customer.

Those are the cards i have been dealt,
that is my hand.

i am willing to play it and
ready to risk everything on it.
And you, my friend?
Wanna bet?

The Confessional Poets

The Confessional poets have always suffered
from the lack of critical intelligence.
The critics called them Confessional because
they revealed their loathing for others:
Daddy, you bastard you;
that sort of thing.

What the critics failed to understand
because they are not very bright, is
how few of them turned the confessional booth
inside out
and confessed their loathing for self,
they did not confess their own sin which is

what confession is all about;
the other is easy.
i am a Confessional poet and my sin
was to betray the love of my daughters
for spiritual gain,
like saint Judas.

I broke my daughters' hearts
by divorcing their mother and then
did it again by divorcing them,
abandoning them to live with a Guru
who was as great as any Master but
i was not fit to carry my daughters' shoes.

Betrayal of Love is the original and only sin

and i have sinned.
That is confession, the rest
is mere complaint.
Daddy, the bastard is me.

Saint Judas

Very few things stir human blood so deeply
as betrayal.
Every life has known it, some many times
and once you have known it you can never
be the same again, but

once you have done it, some delicate mechanism
carefully balanced and crucial in the heart
breaks and can rarely ever be repaired.
From that moment on the brave tick-tock
of the heart measures the seconds of your dying,
not your living.

Like Saint Judas, i betrayed Love.
Raised by 2 drunks, i was well trained to
break my daughters' hearts with divorce and
then by leaving to live with a Guru.
They were 2 Angelic beings sent here
to be broken and betrayed

by their father for spiritual profit,
just like Saint Judas.
Before, life was swift, flew like
young birds raptured in a rising current;
after, the days crept by like dark mourners
grieving the death of a savior.

Saint Judas hanged himself, they say and
i do not doubt it but the joke

was on him; you don't get off that easy:
first he reincarnated as a dog, betrayed
and beaten every day of his life by a drunk
who was his master; then
he came back as a woman with
the same man for a husband;
then as a young king with evil counselors;
then as a child with 2 drunks for parents and
when he was grown, 2 daughters whom he adored,

but he was Saint Judas and he was
required to see it from all sides
and to pay and pay until
he had used up all 30 pieces of silver,
one lifetime per coin; he
could not help himself.

Little Wind and the Death of Barbie

Some time after the divorce, when Little Wind was ten
they moved to Houston. Somehow she had retained
an innocence and purity that can mean trouble when
displayed in this world. The quality of mercy is strained

among schoolchildren who are learning to draw blood
with words and insinuation, to prepare them for what is to come;
Little Wind's Barbie dolls brought on a flood
of such abuse among her new friends, she was struck dumb

with horror and shame. Very soon arrived the fatal day
when she packed her dolls in a box, sold it to a neighbor
woman who haggled and found fault, then sent her away
with a few miserly dollars for her broken heart. The labor

of our lives, once we have been gutted and stripped bare,
is to not take personally the horror we see everywhere.

The Last Time I Hit My Daughter

Little Wind was 5
and i was a broken man
ruined by divorce and barely alive
in one tiny room of a boarding house,

hating what i had become.
One day i swatted Little Wind on her belly
and ordered her into the hall; numb
with old sorrows, i closed the door.

Horror instantly vanquished rage.
i opened the door and she stood there
straight and unflinching; old in her age,
she was the noblest human being i ever saw.

On my knees there my life changed, slowly ceased
its madness; kind daughter arose from ruined beast.

Humbled By Love

You say you had a father once
and though you wished he were a prince
he turned out to be a shameful dunce,
a hopeless idiot bereft of common sense

whose behavior would shame a wild boar?
Well I am one like that, a man whose fear
wounded my daughters. Men like me adore
our children, though we tremble at our

ignorance, are foolish and without grace
in our devotion. But slowly what is gross
in us gives way to the child's fearless embrace
the way a barren plain yields to lush grass.

Though in his arrogance the proud man stumbles,
worship of his child ennobles as it humbles.

The Great Poet Gets His Just Rewards

Dear Red, the letter begins, You have been named
the Honored Poet in the Silver Jubilee Poetry Festival.
A silver chalice with a leaded crystal base and
your name engraved on it Red, will be presented to you
at a special honoring banquet where you will read your poetry
in front of an audience of 1,000 poets,
all there to honor you Red.
And your poem has been selected for our beautiful hardback
Silver Jubilee Prize Poems Anthology; you can
reserve your copy now for $49.99 and as an honored poet
you can get additional copies at a 10% discount.
Should your poem win our $10,000 GRAND PRIZE Red,
your poem will lead off this deluxe, silver-edged volume
containing all of the best poets in the United States.
At the banquet you will share the dias with famous poet
Leonard Nimoy, That's Right! Dr. Spock of Star Trek fame
will be there to honor you Red, and you and he
will share the reading spotlight together Red.
The $10,000 check made out to RED HAWK is waiting for you
to enter our sweepstakes, $10 per poem, 40 line limit, double spaced.
Leonard Nimoy himself will select the GRAND PRIZE winner.
But HURRY! The finest poets in the country
are flocking to Miami and there are only a few rooms left.
See you there!

I was sorry to miss the best flocking poets in the country,
but they would have to go flock themselves
and read their $10 poems before an audience
of 999 including poor Spock,

who never could believe the stupidity of human beings but
must have grown too old for Starship Service and
so he was forced down in a galaxy of $10 aliens where
he is still considered a star and
they will pay him to read his poems until
he has had enough and they beam him up,
weary at last
of the flocking grind.

This Path Is the Path of Suffering

Most people would regard this as utterly insane,
to embark upon a path where suffering is the conscious intent.
They are of course blind to the ability of the human brain
to deny what is right before it, which is the extent

to which suffering composes our daily lives;
whether it be the systematic enslavement and torture
of beasts and children, or the horror which husbands and wives
enact upon one another in the name of marriage, the forfeiture

of our divinity is the result. To see this clearly
is suffering, both in others and in myself which is
the worst kind of suffering, a clarity for which i pay dearly
to see that the real, genuine son-of-a-bitch is

me and no one else. Where seeing self is the Conscious intent,
we are compelled by suffering to go to our knees and repent.

Remorse of Conscience

There is a fearful price that Conscience pays:
the suffering of remorse allows the Soul
to transcend the body's brutal hurtful ways
in order that it might reach a finer goal:

the elevation of kindness above personal interest;
Conscience is the heart of the mature Soul freed
from selfishness. To reach this goal, the Wise suggest
that remorse is merely the immature seed,

Conscience is the mature flowering. i have hurt those
who love me, wounded them in deed and word,
my lack of kindness adding to their woes,
and if i dare to see, my heart is fiercely stirred.

In this hard rocky soil a man labors and he sweats,
harvests kindness from a rich astonishment of regrets.

Too Much Juice

Zeema is old as horses go, sweet
and gentle from a life spent with gentle folk,
an old brood mare with no meanness in her so

she was not prepared for the young stallion they
purchased and brought home to the barn.
He was the youngest of the herd so the others

took it all out on him and he was spooked.
My wife who loves to caress and coo the horses
took one look in his eyes and backed off.

The first night he cornered Zeema near the barn and
kicked her hard, knocked her sprawling
in the dirt, underneath the tractor.

He is the kind the farmers go to weighing
with and without their balls.
Once they take those away,

the gelding dances to a different tune.
Once my juice ran hot like this one's
and i looked for trouble everywhere;

i still have everything i came here with but
banking that fire is the hardest work
anybody could ever wish to do.

It took 2 daughters and a good wife,
2 Gurus and a damned hard life
to keep me from the farmer's knife.

The Value of Necessity

Necessity is the mother of all Work.
Once a human understands the value and the need
of difficult circumstances, she will not shirk
discomfort anymore, but will work until her hands bleed,

wrap them in rags and go back into it again.
Chandrika and i worked the restaurant trade,
slaved in a small hot kitchen for 9-10
hours a day chopping and cutting and when the blade

took off the tip of my thumb that's just how it went:
wrapped it in rags and right back to the grind;
nothing but our daily sweat would pay the rent,
no time for feeling sorry, no room for the reluctant mind.

Necessity is what compels the wolf to take down the moose;
we surrender to God only when we feel the tightening of the noose.

The Ancient Regime

The farm boys of Arkansas drive down to the ships of war
in old trucks, Viet Nam era 35-year-old broken down Dodge trucks
their National Guard units have wired together and kept alive.
The young farm boys believe in their government, believe
they would never be sent into battle wanting, but
too late they find out this war has remote roadside bombs
which blow off arms and legs of those in unarmored trucks,
this war has invisible foes with rocket-propelled-grenades
which penetrate unarmored vehicles. So the clever farm boys
from Arkansas begin to scavenge sheet metal and torches.
They who kept the old Dodge trucks alive by sheer ingenuity

now weld boiler plates, car hoods, tractor doors and
refrigerator walls to the sides and bellies of worn out Dodges
and when they run out of metal, they take off their flak vests
and rope them to the doors of the ruined Dodge trucks,
praying this will save their arms and legs for plowing
when they get back home, if they ever do.
What they do not find out until much later, too late, is that
nothing can protect them from their own ammunition; the
depleted-uranium munitions they use to kill the enemy
kills them as well, only slowly, painfully, an agony of deceit.
Depleted uranium is the generals' great love, it gives them

overwhelming firepower superiority, the unfair advantage which
generals long for at any cost; in this case the cost is
their own farm boys who no longer believe in their government
once they are Gulf War Veterans and they have the sickness:
radiation poisoning comes from exposure to depleted-uranium;

the generals love it because it ignites instantaneously to
5,400 degrees, is 1.7 times denser than Lead, will penetrate
any known armor and vaporizes whatever it hits. In the process,
70% of the uranium is atomized into minute dust particles
and is blown back into the faces of the farm boys who breathe it
like it was dust blowing off of Delta cotton fields, only

this dust gives them cancers, crippling headaches, rashes that bleed
when they scratch, terrible palsies so bad they cannot stand, and
chronic fatigue so they cannot work; those who are lucky die.
There are always more farm boys willing to die, plentiful
as young pigs fattened for the abattoir, willing
to believe any lie because they have to, otherwise
nothing makes sense, their lives are without meaning,
their deaths lack all nobility. Generals do not grieve
their losses; farmers do not grieve their pigs;
they count their profit and call their endless savage war
winning the peace. Repeating a lie often enough

does not make it true.

The Devotee

My neighbor Joan was big which was the reason
the kids called her Moose. No matter the season

she wore low-cut peasant blouses,
the kind that brings young boys out of their houses

like dogs when a feral scent excites the air.
She took no shit, even from her brutal father. Once he yanked her hair

in the yard late at night and she slugged him in the face
so he grabbed and broke her finger. No disgrace

scared her; in fact the tawdry violence inspired her
to such heroic acts that, cowered in the shadows, I admired her

bravery.
Shackled in my own fearful slavery,

I stood in her shadow, wondering if courage could be learned
without walking into the fire, where my friend burned.

The Last Warrior

Geronimo was Apache, a great warrior.
By 1864 the Apache were beaten, however
Geronimo would not surrender with the rest;
instead he took a small band of warriors,
women and children, and headed for Mexico but

it was no good;
they were hunted like dogs by the cavalry,
near starvation and most of the warriors dead, when
Geronimo surrendered to General Miles in Skeleton Canyon.
This is what he said when he handed over his rifle:

Our women have no more milk in their breasts and
there are no more Buffalo on the grasslands.
Your people wipe out everything until
all that is left is human beings.
If you could, you would steal our eyes.

Our children cry for food and there is none.
I am here because the warrior's place is to
stand by the women and children to the last.
I do not surrender; you may kill me and it is
good if you do, but the women and children surrender.

If I am killed, no one should mourn for me.
You people have all the food and I ask you
to share some of it with our people.
As for me, I do not want your food;
I do not want anything you have and

I do not want anything to do with you for
you are death dressed up in a white robe and
I am a dead man already, a ghost
walking among starving children.
There is nothing you can do to me.

And he handed over his rifle.

The Guru's Clever Trap

i cling to the tatter of the Guru's shawl
like a young boy to the hem of his mother's dress.
One lives an individual life until it is all
used up and crumbles beneath the unbearable duress

placed upon it by simple self-observation.
The chinks begin to appear in the stonework and
the mind armors itself for a battle of annihilation
until there is nowhere left for the embattled disciple to stand

except to take refuge beneath the Guru's shawl. It's a neat
trap the Guru sets for us, tempting the psyche with the bait
of self knowledge, which knowledge sends the psyche into retreat
and slowly leads to its cooperating in its own demise. The fate

of the disciple, broken by madness, falls to the Master,
whose skillful means are all that stand between him and disaster.

Why I Don't Have to Act Crazy Anymore

It got me a long way in life,
the crazy routine. It got me
the attention i craved and it kept people
at arm's length which is the way i liked it.
It scared me, the possibility
of a broken heart, so
i was crazy and they
noticed me but kept their distance.

Then i met Mister Lee who is
a lot crazier than i ever had the nerve to be
and a Wise Master as well and
it is the Wisdom which got me because
it is the one thing which
i was never able to fit into my act.

One day Mister Lee was sitting in a cafe
eating chocolate cream pie.
One of His close female disciples,
thinking she was His familiar,
criticized Him for His manners.

He took the chocolate cream pie and
smashed it on top of His head, fudge
and whipped cream running slowly
down into His face.
His disciples sat there horrified,
not so much because every single eye in the place

was on the Master's chocolate face,
but because they suddenly understood
in a way they never had before
the line between respect
and familiarity.
It is that kind of Crazy Wisdom
which got me to come off my act.
I'd rather eat my pie
than wear it.

Been There, Still Am

i have been far down, given
up on myself, been eaten alive with fear,
all self-pity and despair, no love, mad as Lear
on the moor, ruined, broken and driven

to self destruct.
So when the bum approached me on Main Street
and said, "Buddy I'm all fucked
up and don't have anything to eat,"

i dug deep, gave him all the change i had.
He seemed surprised that i didn't hesitate
and thanked me profusely. i don't feel bad
for men like us, consumed with self-hate,

because i know where it can lead.
We only go for God out of hopeless, desperate need.

A Challenge for the Son of God

i am badly damaged, crippled up
and sadly wounded within so that i am
constantly afraid, self-centered
and insensitive to others' feelings, an awful

bore. Yet, you Master are the dear and Lawful
son of God. Your Master made that clear
over and over again.
Jesus, another Lawful son, was said to heal

the lame and sick. Big deal,
that was nothing, a minor barstool trick.
What i propose is that you heal me;
there's a wonder they would talk about

for a thousand years if you could find out
how to make me useful to our Lord.
If the Son of God could make a good disciple
out of a son of a bitch,

that would humble your critics and make you rich.
i stumble because i am blind
and must look to one like you, who is kind
to keep me from falling into a ditch,

where alone and weeping i would surely perish.
Make me something our Lord might cherish.

Our Hearts Are Restless 'Til They Rest In Thee

Religious sentiment is mostly sentimental crap,
the absurd posturing of liars and cheats
who have fallen into the classic liar's trap:
believing that everyone he meets

is an idiot who will be easily fooled
by a line of crap. So any love i claim
for you dear Master is immediately over-ruled
by the fact that a liar by any other name,

including devotee, is still a liar and i am one
to the bone so even i do not trust
such proclamations of undying love. You are the Son
of a great Master and i am just

a lying fool who sneaked into the company of the wise;
the history of my love is told entirely in lies.

Because I Have A Guru

People assume i am a nice guy
and they can lay their awful writing on me
and i will be kind;
they assume i will not mind
reading their dreadful crap and listening by
the hour to their deadly boring story

of how they were abused by life and
had their hearts broken by evil men.
Usually this happens one time
and when i tell them what i think of their rhyme
they go away and never come back again.
Because i have a Guru, people assume i will stand

there and take it like some tired, helpless dunce
but like i said, it usually only happens once.

Confession of A Camp Follower

i am not one of your pretty disciples Master,
nor is there any virtue here: no faithful practice,
no adherence to the Dharma or even so much
as the purchase of a cheap brass trinket
at your merchandise bazaar.
i confess i wave your picture about proudly
before anyone who will stop to look, like
a street whore with a 5-dollar bill.
i hang around on the fringes of your camp
like one of the pack dogs at the edge
of an Indian village, waiting to scrounge
any stray scraps that fall from your table,
leaping upon them with bared fang and
a snarl to keep the others off, then
devouring the smallest crumb from your hand.
But i am not trained so beware,
i will bite,
i will pee on your lodge pole and
lick myself shamelessly in the middle
of any Sacred space. And yet, and
yet, there you are dear Master, oh
beautiful Sir you rub my belly, you
caress my face and you say to me,
Good boy, oh good boy.

i lick the dust from your feet.

Everywhere I Turned It Was No Good

At home it was alcohol nightmares
every goddam day and night. If
they were not screaming, cursing and
hurting one another, then my parents
unleashed the hellfire of their dying
upon my sister and i with fist and curse
and the dark despair of the damned.
It was the only way they knew to love us
was to break our hearts as
the world had broken theirs utterly.

So i went to public school with great hope
that somewhere in the hell of this world
there was a place free from the horror but
it was not to be.
There among the scholars of this world
dwelled the bullies, those damned souls
for whom torture is the way they teach and
torment is the instrument of their wisdom. But

for every bully there must be a victim and
it was given to me to be their lamb in whom
they took great delight in the slaughter.
Grade school was bad enough but in high school
i met the King of the Bullies and
as the arrow finds its inevitable mark
he found me.
i loved a woman he fancied and i loved her
with a precious innocence and a depth of feeling

like the wind which stirs leaf, branch and root
in the storms of summer leaving nothing
unmoved by its terrible beauty.

And he chased me from her beautiful lips,
he cowed me and sent me brokenly away
from her dark eyes and black hair because
i believed there was nothing in this world
worse than a beating.
It takes a terrible price to learn otherwise and

so i grew and paid
seeing no relief anywhere, at home or school or
in church where the damned sang and prayed
but nothing changed in their lives at all and
at night they went home and fell on their knees
before their drink and cursed the beautiful God
in their children. Everywhere i turned
it was no good and
so i assumed was i,
no good
for anything but a beating and the sorrow
of the fallen leaf, the dread
of the uprooted sapling and

so i grew and paid and
so it is with me still, a frog
among the lilies, a lone bird tossed
in the storm, a poet for whom

these words are the last best hope
that the damned may arise and walk
among the great standing trees whose

limbs at night hold the very shining
stars which must one day die as
we all must
having stood up to our beating and paid
with the utmost farthing
for the right to inherit the wind.

The Man With the Brass Spittoon

One day Papa Ram Dass and Mother Krishnabai
were sitting together in Darshan
with a hundred disciples.
Papa was chewing betel
and spitting with great accuracy
into an elegant brass spittoon
sitting near Him on the platform:

no miss, no mess, He
hit it every time.
Suddenly,
before anyone could move to stop him,
a wild looking devotee
rushed from the audience,
grabbed the spittoon,

and drank down its contents
in one long gulp.
The audience gasped in disbelief
and many of course were
immediately envious that they had
neither the courage nor
the personal power

to have done such a thing.
But courage and power
are never enough when
used only for personal gain.
Papa made that clear; when

the man left, He turned to Krishnabai smiling.
This man is a dangerous man, He said and

He let another one fly at the spittoon;
precise, accurate, He
hit it perfectly
dead center,
working up a new supply
for the next fool
with a thirst.

Part iĩi. The Beggar: between 2 worlds

"...Mindful among the mindless,
Awake while others dream,
Swift as the race horse
He outstrips the field.

By watching
Indra became king of the gods.
How wonderful it is to watch,
How foolish to sleep.

The beggar who guards his mind
And fears the waywardness of his thoughts
Burns through every bond
With the fire of his vigilance.

The beggar who guards his mind
And fears his own confusion
Cannot fail.
He has found the way to peace."

            – Buddha, *The Dhammapada*, 11.

The Beggar

Dearest, it's not my character to beg,
but there is nothing else that I can do
because I'm broken like a fragile egg
and so I come on bended knee to you

and plead with you dear Master do not make
a unified and stable man of me,
the kind who nothing in this world can break
because he has an inner unity

and has attained to oneness with you Lord.
Keep me ignorant, wretched, asinine;
surely one fool like me you can afford,
whose bad example makes the rest to shine

and if all others got to heaven before you
Beloved, who would be left to adore you?

I Want to Die Like Mary Lou

Mary Lou was my guardian and spiritual mother,
kind and generous, though aging brought out another
darker side: wracked by disease and the ravages of drink
she appeared to be headed for the very brink
of madness. i would not have laid even a small bet
that she would be able to die well, and yet
as she lay dying she summoned a hidden strength
that many people have gone to any length
to find, and failed. She became strong and clear
as the hooded Huntsman drew near
and though she labored long in great pain,
she refused to complain.
There are any number of ways to measure a saint;
one way would be the death without complaint.

Elijah Dies at Home

We know so little of how this world works;
much worth doing is not done in one lifetime. Death
makes length of stay mean nothing because it lurks
behind each brief breath.

Due to Meningitis, Elijah only stayed 13 months here
but he was born with a Guru, Father and Mother
were devoted disciples, and he was raised without fear.
Because his life was so full, its length does not bother

me at all; he will find the spiritual life again
at his next birth because he was allowed
to die at home in his parents' arms, not how and when
the hospital decided. Because they were not cowed

by death, Elijah got a full and complete taste
of the deeper life; that timeless path knows no haste.

Something Given, Something Taken Away
(for George)

Age diminishes us piece by piece
even as it builds something within, gives
with one hand, shortens our lease
on the body with the other as long as it lives.

To get at George's lung, the oncologist took a rib today.
What the hell, we've got 24, 12 pairs
so i guess it's no big deal you could say.
24-23 more or less, who cares,

but each mortal piece, no matter how small
reminds us that the body is on short-term loan.
We can remember then that this body is not all
there is of us; something much finer can be known

not directly, but as wind is known by the flutter in the trees,
or as unseen love brings a strong man to his knees.

George Makes A Sacrifice for Art

George is a painter; they took one of his ribs today,
part of his cancerous lung as well. The rib interests me
because i wonder, do they just throw it away
or can it be used for something? It has real possibility:

you could carve it like they do whale bone,
make a knife handle, beads, dice, a curved totem out of it,
or you could paint it real fancy George, call it high-tone
art; now there would be a man who's no bullshit,

he puts all of himself into his art;
or your wife, the potter, could make a handle for a pot.
Hell, you've already given her your heart
so a rib is nothing, why not?

But for God's sake don't just toss the rib aside;
God only needed one for Adam to make himself a bride.

In His Dying Grace

As for George, he is dying but
slowly and with a tender grace.
George is good at dying. For him
it is just what is happening, no more
and not less than just this.
Without malice or pity he is

laying it down.
We gather in his dying light, all of us
old friends in love with laughter and
George comes in carrying apple pie. I had
bacon and eggs for breakfast, he says as if
the cavalry crossing the creek were

such a thing of beauty in itself that
it did not matter
they came for dying,
sabers rattling against their flanks, horses
moving in unison like cancer cells through blood; And
the bacon was crisp, eggs over easy, he says.

The Fool Curses the Law of Entropy

It goes on.
George is dying, one Sun around whom
one small band of planets circled but
all Suns grow old and die,
the planets go cold and fly off
into the dark with nothing left
to hold them in place.

Still, as the light makes its falling arc
across the face of night
a thousand stars are born
and shed their tender mercies upon the dark.
One falls away,
another dawns to light the way
and though we wish that it would stay,
night always covers up the day.

So it is foolish to grieve his dying,
like the tree mourning the loss
of a single leaf.
i may be a damn fool for crying
but if Jesus could weep upon His cross
i can show my grief.

Damn the stars for not weeping
and for keeping on
when one among them falls into the dark
and its elegant individual spark goes out.
i am not a star and

i will curse death for going too far,
torturing George Bireline with a raging storm of pain
when he deserves a rainbow and a gentle rain;

even if the darkness is needed,
don't let the passing of the dear day go unheeded.

The Paintings Don't Tell the Whole Story

They say in each creation, the artist dwells
and thus is granted a fragile immortality
amidst the various critical hells
of waning taste and art world venality,

so here are George's remains hung upon the walls
for all to see, and here his bright glory calls
to us like a flower garden in full dazzling bloom
before the first frost delivers its doom.

Yet there is no hint here of the grace
with which he died,
how he struggled each day to take his place
before the canvas, stick to steady hand, wife by side,

and how he swallowed the awful drugs without complaint
for 15 pain-free minutes to stand and paint.

The Art Critics

Friend of mine runs the art department
at the local college and his painting class
just finished a big mural project
on the back wall of the bookstore
where the concrete loading dock stands,

where the trucks come in and
unload the refuse, the leavings
of the dead poets and writers who
once had talent but now write the
critical studies and edit the anthologies.

So today i went over to admire the mural,
a pretty thing done by students with some talent
and i thought that it was not bad,
all things considered but then
as i was leaving i saw it over in the corner,

a neat, undisturbed pile of dog leavings,
not fresh but with the smell intact.
Sometimes life delivers a kind of
sweet perfection.
i couldn't help it, i laughed

and laughed thinking, Ahhh
the art critics,
they are everywhere and
their leavings always
smell the same.

Mourning's Progress
(for Jen)

The early light in his painting studio brushes shadow
onto the wall nearest her small bed which
she has set up there because it is the one place
in the vast emptiness of the deserted house where
he is still most alive.

The light fondles the paint splotched wall,
figures and shadows the dozens of torn
magazine photos and ads he placed there
to remind him of the angle of her neck, the
shadow of her breasts when she bends

to pour herself her morning tea, places the delicate cup
on his stack of New Yorkers, the soft yellow light
caressing her white hair like his waking hand once did.
Early morning, the blessed oblivion of sleep withdrawn,
she must reassemble the reasons to go on, why

it makes any sense to move to her own clay studio
and throw one more pot, when nothing lasts.
We take everything for granted until the loss
of one central item calls all the rest
into question,

that loss being the light which illuminates
each of the things of this world from within.
He was that light for her, and now she begins
the elemental discourse with a thing unseen

as the shadow inches across her wall

not of its own accord but moved by the
unseen essence of the Sun hidden from her view
just out of reach on the other side of the glass;
it is the fleeting but still visible remains
of a journey of light-years, millions of miles

from the last sheer stunning wordless infinite touch
of his dying hand upon her face, the light
passing from his eyes onto this wall where
her gaze rests at the intersection of duty and despair
until she rises, bone china in her hands and

begins again the ancient holy journey
back into her flesh, the light
now bathing the floor at her feet, her cheek
lit from the side as if a painter had placed her just so,
that he might never forget her face.

We Do Not Grieve For Death

What fills the void where once a man stood tall,
or does the mighty Oak come crashing down
and if there is no soul to mourn its fall,
it leaves no mark, it makes no mortal sound?

Then we will grieve the passing of our friend
and raise a cry to pierce and rend the breast;
let our voice join with angels to attend
his death and sing him to his gentle rest.

The Wise make an ally of their death;
with every precious breath they die
and make a prayer upon each dying breath,
at once both plentiful, and in dreadful short supply.

We do not grieve for death, that common whore,
we grieve for what we held and hold no more.

When Grief Transforms the Heart

His absence endures,
the way a pillow holds for a moment
the impression of a head, or for years
the heart bears the memory of its torment

at his passing.
Sometimes in the teeth of the fiercest storm
there is a momentary calm; just when she is missing
him most profoundly, her flesh recalls the weight of his arm

thrown across her in their dreaming sleep
and she jerks upright in her solitary bed
to see if he is there, but he escapes
before she can even remember to be sad.

Comes a point in mourning when grief transforms the heart;
as Lotus springs from mud, a quiet joy arises from the hurt.

Old Love Know Best

Old love knows best
upon which bed to lay its fate to rest;
it is not hurried by the changing seasons,
nor rushed, though reason gives a thousand reasons.

It is not marked by anger nor by dread;
by patience and by kindness it is known.
Its root goes deep, beyond the flesh and bone,
so it alone remains when life has fled.

Old love flows free, not bound by time or space;
its blessings fall upon the hour and the day,
and on the years which swiftly pass away
but it alone escapes Death's cold embrace

because Death has no hold on it, no sway.
Death only rules the dust; old love does not decay.

Beauty is Dearest When it is Gone
(for Chinaski)

Death is the mother of beauty,
Wallace Stevens said.
Is adoring it while it's still alive our duty,
instead of valuing it too late when it's dead,

or is it that the lover left alone in the cold bed
knows beauty truest by its absence? She can toss
about the idea of it endlessly in her head,
but never deeply feel its loss;

only in that broken feeling can she understand the cost
of beauty in this place where we are born to die;
only then does she truly value and adore what she has lost.
Thought alone does not make beauty; we must cry

and in our deepest broken weeping,
beauty is awakened from her inner sleeping.

In the Stone and Boneyard

It puzzles me why men care
what happens to the bones
after they are stripped bare
of breath, why they need stones

to mark the spot where nothing lies,
a brain devoid of content, no mind
that thinks nor mouth which cries
out for sanctuary. When the cold wind

moves among the stones, no shiver
is forthcoming there, and when that long lost name
engraved upon the stone is called, no quiver
of recognition in the trees and neither fame

nor blame awakens the flesh from its rot.
What's left of you is dirt, when you are not.

Boom or Bust

Today, unshaven and half sick, i walk slowly
home from the grocery store through the boneyard
and as i come out of the trees and tall grass
i see them,

cars lined up along one pathway,
a small crowd gathered under a green canopy,
fresh dirt in a pile alongside,
another one down the hole.

I pause for a moment there in the tall grass.
In the giant Oak tree in the middle of the boneyard,
something has gotten the attention of the Crows
and they are singing a chorus

in praise of the newly dead.
One shrieks and dives and that is when
i see the 2 of them over in one corner of the yard,
one man leaning on a shovel, the other

inside an idling Bobcat dozer, waiting.
They are smoking and laughing, the Crows
wheel in and among the stones,
and i carry the groceries on home.

In the boneyard everyone is equal,
everyone has their assigned hole and
whether the economy is boom or bust
the grave diggers and the Crows

always turn a profit.

Rain Beats Down on the Last Leaf of Memory

All day Fall rain blew across the plowed field
and i walked in its mud, trees along one side,
down to the creek behind.
Near creek's edge where the plow stopped i kneeled
in the fallen wet leaves, where the Copperheads hide
along the bank. Something laying rain-shined

there caught my eye.
Lifting one leaf i found a large arrow point, chert
or Arkansas Novaculite, wet white stone
still stuck in a fragment of human bone
and i wondered kneeling there who this point hurt,
who shot and why, who of us came here to die?

All that's left of anyone beneath the fallen leaf
is stone and bone; gone the triumph, gone the grief.

The Clay Is In the Fire
(for Natalie)

Life burns hotter,
the older we get.
Take Alex, who is 17 and is now
in terrible conflict with his mother who
once was his dearest companion.

She tells him what to do over and over and
he refuses;
she nags him and
he tells her to shut up. She is bright and
eventually, though her heart is breaking,

she will learn what the potter knows:
as long as the clay is soft and wet
you can mold and shape it any way you wish
and it will respond
to the slightest pressure

from your thumb, but
once the clay
is in the fire,
the potter's work is done and
it all depends upon the quality of the clay

and the delicacy of the form now,
whether the pot cracks and shatters
or is strong and solid,
able to hold
the water.

All That is Solid Melts Into Air
(for the Marx Brothers: Karl & Groucho)

The mightiest fall when their time has come,
the brave man one day will cease to dare,
and the most eloquent speaker will be struck dumb;
all that is solid melts into air.

So what is there left to measure a man
if such virtues as these can get him nowhere?
How will they remember him, those of his clan
if all that is solid melts into air?

The wise have long argued which virtue's most dear,
but of all put together no matter how rare,
on this they agree and are perfectly clear:
when all that was solid melts into air,

nothing else matches it, even by half;
let him be most blessed who made his friends laugh.

The Development of Attention

We are caught by every vagrant breeze,
our lives a constant distraction from what is
right in front of us, our vision

always on tomorrow so that
we miss the glory of today.
But there are the few who understand

that the doorway to the Divine
lies in the cultivation of a present-Attention,
a facility for seeing what is

right in front of me.
Louis Agassiz, the Harvard naturalist,
was once asked what he had done

with his summer vacation.
I traveled far and wide,
he said. How far, he was asked?

I got
half way across
my back yard, he replied.

The Farmer Plowing His Field

They report that Icarus drowned but
i do not think so.
No, i believe
he landed hard, broken

and dying in early spring
in a field being plowed by
a poor woman, her husband
in front of her yoked to the plow
the way Icarus was yoked to his father's dream,

the farmer strapped in and stooped
to the grinding, merciless work,
the hot sun beating him to death as he
makes his way through the sweating air

pulling the heavy weight of his dream
on his sore and ruined back.
A motion in the corner of the eye
catches them mid-breath;
the sheep at the edge of the field

look up and the woman stops in her tracks;
he is looking down at the dirt
which catches his sweat like pooled blood
so it is the heavy Thump!

out of nowhere
which stops his breathing.

First he turns to question his wife,
then follows the frozen horror of her gaze
to the center of the plowed furrow,

to the heap of feathers, to the
barest tremble of air like
the last breath of his youngest child
as she lay dying in his helpless arms.

He looks at his wife and without a word
they unstrap themselves
and gather it in their arms,
take a shovel and do
what they have always done:

bury the dream,
shoulder the harness,
plow the field, seed,
begin again.

The Anasazi Ruins Are Not Ruined

Just north of Prescott, AZ and well hidden in the foothills
beneath Granite Mountain are the remains of a small
Anasazi settlement maybe 1,000 years old.
Sturdy stone walls fill in the gaps between large boulders,
stretch like a spine along the ridge and snake their way
down along the humps and ridges and plateaus
to the sheer cliff edge and the immense boulder field
which slopes 300 feet to a dry creek bed.
The walls are still standing there, as silent and
dependable, as responsible and protective as they were

the day they were built.
There is no mortar or mud to hold the stones;
they have been worked so they have flat sides,
then they are stacked, careful trim solid stacks with
smaller worked stones and pieces for leverage and balance
to fill in the spaces and make the surface level.
Dozens of people, men, women and children,
lifted and carried stones to the masons who
chipped and chinked, then to the wall builders
who placed and rearranged and filled in and

now i sit here with my back against their wall
a thousand years old, sweat running into my shirt
and onto the stones where it mixes with their
dried sweat salt. The wall does not budge, it
holds me up. It is a real place and
i am not there long before i am stone age, which
does not mean brute stupid but clear and smart,

wise to stone and the placement of stone, wise
to water, the movement and containment of it,
bodily intelligent, no wasted movement in the heat;

i think in stone, not in words, lay my body down,
blink once and am covered over by starry night.
A thousand years is a stone's throw from here,
but the stones are indifferent,
they do as they are placed to do and
do not protest as they are worn by wind,
smoothed and diminished by rain,
aged by heat and freezing. They are made
to lay down their lives.
That is what they do.

Gone the incidental hand which placed them,
dust at their base; gone
the bodies which lay here, coupled, spermed,
rooted, lived, died. The stones
shrug off the brief shadow of the animal
which changes its clothes and
makes fire because it lacks fur to cover itself.
What we know of time is its motion;
stones know its geology. They are patient, they
know how to wait.

What i Remember of the Good Times

Nothing will ever equal my daughters or my wife;
Little Wind and Rain Drop and Moonlight are
all the luck any human being will ever need.
So there is that, and it is enough.

But below that on the list of good things
many might place sex. I won't kid you,
sex has been good to me; women have blessed me
and i have laid with some extraordinary ones.

Also the Little Smoke and the Medicine pipe
were good to me, likewise the students i have taught.
They were all as good as it gets but
just below my daughters and my wife is

that day in Chaco Canyon when we hiked for hours
in the blistering Sun across a tough dry stony land,
followed the old footworn paths, traced with our fingers
the petroglyphs carved in the hard stone,

climbed breathless through the tight spiral chimney
to the top of the bluff, walked the high ledge,
went 4 miles out to the last outpost, then back
and finally made our way to our campsite,

hot, dry, worn, exhausted and there
you pulled our only 2 beers out of the cooler
and we uncapped those cold bottles. My God,
those beers were good.

Carlos Castaneda is Dead

He died of liver cancer
but the strangest thing about his last years
was the vague sense of searching about him.
He gave occasional workshops, often

called at the last moment to which
dozens, sometimes hundreds of people came and
much of what he said there
is lost to us,

but what is recorded
is the answer he gave a woman
near the time he died, when she asked him
how to find a spiritual life:

Every night sit in a chair, he said,
and remember that you and everyone you love
are going to die, in no particular order,
unpredictably;

do this
every night and
soon enough you will
have a spiritual life.

Why the White Man Will Never Win

In the days when $25 meant something,
Hollywood hired 30 Sioux for one of its
epic western movies and promised them
$25 a day to act in the movie, with a

bonus of $50
if any of them fell off his horse
during filming of the battle scenes.
So the 30 Lakota Sioux are supposed to

attack a wagon train,
yelling and screaming. As they
approach the last wagon in line
a single settler sticks his skinny arm out

and fires a single shot from his pistol.
All 30 Indians
immediately fall off their horses
onto the ground.

Boasting Is A Small, Weak Death

i am a boastful man, a fearful little braggart
for whom no triumph is good enough to dare
let it speak for itself. What gives me Heart
is the Athabascan, who spearhunt Grizzly Bear.

The Athabascan hunters are wise. They understand
what bragging is. They call it the Hungry Ghost,
an energetic force which drains a man and
consumes his Being when he is moved to boast.

One Athabascan hunter alone with a spear
hunts a Grizzly and if he ever kills one
they say he has learned how to manage his fear.
He never speaks to anyone of the kill, by tradition,

a test to keep his mouth shut and not lie his way to hell;
this struggle conserves his force and helps him die well.

Lord, Where Can I Hide From the Dark Angel?

We are the victims of the information age,
where inevitably even the Holocaust becomes a text
and we wait in horrified fascination for what comes next;
it didn't happen unless we see it on the page

where the mind engages in its endless distraction
from real life, as if death were a theory
which thinking can avoid. Our heart grows weary
when robbed of deep feeling, its only satisfaction.

We are diminished if the mind is the sole focus
of our attention. Words are no substitute for rage,
no theory can deter the ravages of old age;
naming it does not stop the locust

from devouring the corn,
or the rabbit in the fox's mouth from being torn.

Become As Passers-By

Everything disappears
and rapidly.
The Black Bear
moving through the woods slowly, who

stops to eat the berries and to shit,
who makes 2 miles maybe in an hour if
he doesn't find a field of flowers to roll in
which cuts down his speed considerably,

he disappears and rapidly; the Monarch butterfly
fluttering through my campsite makes
half a mile an hour unless she
finds a leafy branch above the stream

like now, and stays there, wings pulsing,
for 25-30 minutes as life goes by and
soon it disappears, and rapidly; or
there is the fool in his camp chair

sitting by the stream watching
the bear, the butterfly, the fish and the
days go by and disappear and if he's lucky
he makes 100 yards in a week

and at that pace he sees all of his life pass
before his eyes because he is going
slow enough that everything passes him and
he passes nothing except

occasionally gas,
and out,
and
away.

All Form Is Emptiness

Today they pulled out my first bad tooth,
cracked in 2 pieces from living and aging.
The first one gives you a moment's reflection,

you consider the body's mortality, the futility
of its stand against aging, the slow retreat,
the inevitability of its decline. My tongue

cannot let the gap alone. There they are,
1-2-3-4, all soldiers standing straight, then
the empty hole, one down and gone, corpse discarded,

nothing left but the emptiness, over and over again.
Of course it gets easier the older we get. The next one
may appear in a bite of sandwich, the lone

bloody tooth, the one after that while flossing, but
the first one is the traffic-stopper, the warning flare:
something has changed and will never be the same;

wisdom teeth do not confer wisdom, and even though
they are called permanent teeth,
nothing here is;

all form is merely emptiness wearing a 2-dollar suit.

The Journey Into Old Age

With the splitting and yanking of my first ruined tooth,
i realize that the path i wander has rounded a curve
and the angle is now a steep descent into the dark woods,
whereas before was the climbing towards light.
Now is the twilight, the kindness and the embrace

of ignorance, the soft quietude of the solitary hunter.
There is no ignorance like that of a man who knows
himself and sees clearly that beyond this, nothing
can be known for certain except that in the most
ordinary way, he is nothing; this nothing can be known.

Old age is the winter of the gathering storm, the howl
held under the breath just shy of hearing, the blind chill
beneath the flesh like a dark root cellar under the floor;
the trick is to remain standing and moving forward though
the lure is to lie down and rest.

The warrior most difficult to defeat is the one
who fights the slow retreat; become empty
as the brown river reed cut from the shore mud
which makes a haunting melody, such a fine pleading
for mercy when the night has been unkind;

it rends the veil between the longing of this world
and the impossible singing.

Up In Smoke

My wife and i are walking the streets
late at night in a gentle rain when
we come around a corner in the dark and

there are the remains of a big house on fire,
the remnants of ordinary lives pushed into a
nice neat pile, a big dozer sitting empty nearby,

everyone gone home, even the firemen,
the blaze low and eerie there in the firelight
where this morning people had lived out

their own kind of ordinary madness in a
big house on a nice street in a little town.
We stop and watch the fire as the gentle rain

falls on what remains of our lives, on what
we could save and what we had to let go.
Smoke drifts out over the street like

a little shadow moving across the body and
there are no stars to light the way, the Moon
does not shine as our lives go up in smoke.

She turns to me and hugs me, we
walk the rest of the way
holding hands in the rain,

one good reason to go on.
All you need
is one.

The Promise of Sex

It seemed to promise everything when i was young,
as if a woman's scented bush, her mouth, her
glistening undulate serpentine tongue,
the mute nostril ecstacy of longing, were the
gateway to the fecund fields of heaven,
the only fruit which could satisfy.

And yet, the best sex i ever had i did not penetrate,
did not come: once a woman straddled my lap facing me,
her skirt around her waist, her blouse half open
and we stroked each other's backs and breasts
for hours, our tongues inside each other's mouths
and she kissed me so hard my lips were bruised

for days and she put her hand down my pants and
held me while she bruised my lips and i tell you,
that was as good as it ever got;
the other time a woman took me out on a dark balcony
and kissed me with soft full thick lips and long tongue
and when she took my tongue in her mouth she

sucked and held it there for nearly 20 minutes while
she took my hand and moaned it up under her skirt
where she wore no panties and her moan lasted
the whole 20 minutes, both of us in a frenzy of lust
like no other i had ever known. Those 2 moments
were the best, all foreplay and promise. And yet,

better than all of those times put together is you

bringing me a bowl of carrot-potato soup,
sitting on the floor beside me, your
dear white head against my leg, holding
my foot, pressing and rubbing the tired arch,
saying, Dearest. Just that, nothing more.

Sex and Good Looks

We live in the great consumer society and
what they are selling is the dream and
the dream is made up of sex and good looks so
we all buy it, how
can we do otherwise? We buy it
and it drives us crazy because

no matter how good the sex is,
and good sex is rare, they never
tell you that, but even then it does not
have staying power;
you can't sustain the life of a garden
by constantly dumping fertilizer on it,
burns it up. And good looks

don't last, they belong to the advertisers.
Now i live with the best woman i have ever known;
we take long walks together and
hold hands everywhere we go,
even in bed.
This is what i love, long walks and holding hands.
i am 60 and the sex and good looks
are peddling flowers on the avenue of broken dreams
but you can't tell that to anybody and expect
they will understand.

The dream dies hard because it is sold hard
and the entire lie depends upon us buying it.
You can't chase the dream if you're walking and
you can't grab for it
if you're holding someone's hand.

Why I Am Faithful

She is gone 2 weeks in the mountains
of North Carolina and i am alone in the house.
i do not intend for this to be one of those sappy poems,
i am not sentimental in that way and

poems like that disgust me. But
she has ruined me for other women, i must
look away even from the young pretty ones
which the campus is crawling with. She has

ruined me and it was not with sex but
with kindness, and friend
that is the worst kind.
If they get you with sex,

there is always another hot one, they are
on every street corner, in every bar
giving it away, waiting
for the next one to come along and

that kind come and they go.
No. Real kindness is different; there are
so few of them in this world that
if the whimsical God smites you with

that kind of dumb luck, then
you have got to change your life or
it will get away from you like
a little shadow flying across the grass and

once you have lost something like that friend,
the days are endless, the nights
a muted cry of despair, so no matter
how pretty and long of leg they are,

i look the other way.

Drinks Her Fill

Time is without remorse, cares nothing
for your dear hand sweetly on my cheek,
your lips a momentary wellspring of desire

against my hair; it moves
without sentiment towards our dying
the way a hungry wolf tracks its prey.

Time leaves its track upon our flesh, like
the wolf's paw in river mud, as it presses us
ever onward into the blue emptiness.

And yet, the mark of your tenderness
is subtler, far softer; and yet
it leaves a thin trail across the heart,

such a faint whisper of longing
upon the ceaseless wind that
even the wolf

bending at the river's edge
to slake her thirst, blood
upon muzzle and fang, pauses

and looks around her
at the sudden hush, the
infinite pause

in the infinite motion, then
bends,
drinks her fill.

These Thoughts That Are Running Through Our Heads

They always change, are not trustworthy, yet
we stake our lives on them, the heart's death-knell;
we take them as our selves and we forget
just who we are; blindly we obey though
they take us down the alleyways of hell.
Into terrible suffering we go,

until one day we see the dreadful wrong
that they do in our name. We see that these
sirens we're in love with sing our death song.
They are never what they appear to be:
they are like a woman you love to please,
until one dark day you find out that she

has slept with evil men and is their whore,
and then you do not want her anymore.

The Weeping of Women Is the Only Dharma We Need

No mother ever profited from war;
only men profit, women weep.
That alone is enough to condemn the enterprise;
what makes women weep is not worth the doing.

There are far worse ways for a man to plan
the course of his actions and the direction of his life
than to avoid at all costs
that which causes women to weep.

I have caused women to weep.
My Mother wept at my cruel treatment of her,
my lovers wept repeatedly
when one by one i turned my back on them,

the mother of my children wept at my insensitivity and
my daughters wept, oh merciful Lord,
oh shameful fool, how my daughters wept
at my ignorance, my sore disgrace.

The tears of women have brought me to my knees
and blessed my heart in their sweet forgiveness,
they have bathed my heart in their tears and dried it
with their hair, breathed upon it and made it live;

what makes women weep is not worth the doing.

Being Right Is the Last Consolation of Ignorance

To Awaken is to question every single thing
which is received as knowledge and to do so
ruthlessly until ideas can be verified by concrete
experience. Otherwise i am enslaved by belief and sing
another's song like the Mockingbird who, though
his song be beautiful, is doomed to repeat

a borrowed tone,
an echo from one who has already flown
away. Questioning belief places one squarely alone
in the vastness of the unknown,

where inquiry can serve as a piercing light
in the Soul's dark night.
To question the very self, to doubt its airtight
certainty is to abandon the consolation of being right.

Family Values

When I was a kid I loved Westerns best,
especially the ones where Gary Cooper
was the sheriff, a strong lone brave
good man against terrible odds, a man

completely unlike my father.
There was always a beautiful woman,
sometimes tough like Coop, often not,
but never in doubt about

who she loved. He made her laugh.
She might go so far
as to leave on the train without him,
but she always came back.

And Coop never flinched from
what he had to do.
He strapped them on and
went to face his death

without a trace of fear.
I walked out of there feeling brave,
as if the world made sense
and goodness always triumphed.

When I got home
my father was beating my mother,
no sheriff
anywhere in sight,

no beautiful woman
laughing,
no train
heading out of town.

Good Friends are Blood Relations That You Choose
(for Les Murray)

The first family arises from the gene pool
and may or may not meet the Soul's need
for naked, intimate company. From the hard School
of life the second comes, those few whom our greed,

fear, anger and sorrow do not drive away,
who by their astonishing and unexpected devotion,
through total breakdown of self and dream, still stay;
they alone form the Soul's family, its teeming ocean

of primal life, the vast salt womb
from which simple uncomplicated Being arises,
that which is true in us and survives our body's doom.
The Soul is revealed through real friendship, surprises

with its passion, unselfish love and generosity,
but it also has a wolf's power and a wolf's wild ferocity.

The One Thing You Can Put Your Money On & Never Lose

What has saved me is, i never followed the crowd,
at first because they wouldn't have anything to do
with me and then because the older i grew
the more i understood that where there is loud

noise and bright lights that is no place for art.
The poem is made in the solitude of the heart,
alone with the sorrows of the day,
the crowd out of hearing and far away.

The crowd always goes for the latest brief flash,
suckered by fashion and the sickness of fame.
But once the bright star is reduced to mere ash,
the solitary poet will still be steady in his flame

because he stayed focused and true to his song;
go opposite the crowd and you'll never go wrong.

The Compassionate Saint

Sitting here late into the night
working at the poems, i get up and
go to the kitchen for a drink of water.

I turn on the light and there he is,
one of the giant roaches which
come with the territory in Arkansas.

All of a sudden years of spiritual practice
sitting on the meditation cushion in the morning dark
sends a rush of compassion through me and

while the world is in flames, nations
are bombing one another, terrorists are
strapping bombs to their bodies and walking

into crowded cafes,
pulling the pin without remorse, and
brutal tyrants are crucifying the innocent

in the name of whatever gods are
currently most useful to them,
i let the roach scurry under the toaster and

i do not pursue it for the kill. And
i used to think that meditation
was not useful.

The Days When the Wild Dogs Strike

This is a day when the wild dogs strike
and that is nothing but a failure of nerve.
It was a day like this when Pollack hit the curve
and was thrown headfirst into a tree, like

this when Hemingway put down his juice
and picked up the shotgun. Nerve is a gift,
the grace of God, which can vanish in one swift
flash: laughter in the throat replaced by a noose,

so we are left bereft and gasping for air.
Once the nerve to go on is gone, then come the wild
dogs ravenous for blood. It is said Saint Joan smiled
as the flames crept up her flesh and devoured her hair;

she never lost her nerve. Some few go strong to the end:
the rare artist, the brave woman, the heroic friend.

Why I Write Poetry

i don't write for you;
i used to write for you because
i cared very much what you thought of me and
i hoped you'd buy my books and
give me your prizes and make me famous and
prove how much you loved me but
i don't write for you anymore;
none of that worked.

i don't write for her;
i used to write for her because
i wanted her to come close and take my hand
up under her skirt where she was naked and
i wanted her to lie down with me and beg me
to do anything i wanted to her, anything but
i don't write for her anymore;
none of it ever worked.

i don't write for money or prizes or fame or
sex or love; i don't write to sell books or
get in the million little magazines who want me
to pay them $20 for their contest to see who
the most desperate whore is. It's the only way
i ever got screwed for poetry and a handjob
is better and cheaper.
i tried to change how i wrote so that
the bastards would change their minds about me.
They never did and never will so

now i write to keep the bastards from changing me;
i write because if i didn't, i would pick up a gun and
come after you, and when i found you i would
show no mercy, so you'd better be glad that
i am writing to save your life, otherwise
these lines would be bullets and i would be
shoving them one by one into the chamber and
i know where you live.

Why Go On?

After you have written so many poems,
so many years, so many books unread
by so many people you begin to ask
the question:
Why go on writing the poems, why
put down one more line which will disappear
into the endless heaps of forgettable verse
waiting to fuel the fires of hell, waiting
like a lost child in a train station for someone,
anyone to come along and take its hand?

Well, i will tell you that today i read where
this year's Pulitzer went to a poet i know,
a poet whose work is impenetrable, impossibly
difficult and embarrassing to understand
for an idiot like me. His poems
are loved by the scholars and the NY Review of Books
who do not work an 8-hour day, work sick and
hurt because the children are hungry and

if they do not show up there is no pay and no
rent money or beer or shoes and socks and
if those tired broken men ever once read
a single poem it better not be the Pulitzer winner's
because 3 lines into it they will throw the book
across the room, cursing, bile rising; they will
swat the kid, pop a beer, turn on the TV and
search for the Handcuffed-in-a-Cage-No-Rules-
Death-Match-Wrestling-Championship

and never pick up a book of poems again
as short as they live.
i am writing for the million-to-1-shot,
the main slim chance,
the impossible odds that the wife will be
on her period or gone for bridge with the girls,
nothing on TV even worth going to sleep behind,
kids at their grandparents,
no more beer and no money to get some, so
he picks up a book of poems out of desperation:

let him turn to this poem, something
he understands, something that does not make him feel
stupid all over again, worthless all day long, used
up like on the assembly line, let him
turn to this poem and say, Fucking right, and
then read the next one until sleep,
blessed sleep comes again to his broken chair.
This one
is for you.

How to Read A Poem

We are consumed by the consumer mentality
which infects us in so many ways that
we do not even know we are sick.
Our emptiness makes us greedy
so we can no longer feel the delicate line

between need and avarice.
The young man comes up to me thinking
he is paying me a compliment.
i read your entire book
in one sitting, he says

and i am ashamed for us all.
If there is anything of value to be had
in the poem
it must be savored like delicate wine
not gulped down like a tired woman

with a tumbler of gin; it must be
tenderly touched like the delicate fine
hairs along a sweet woman's thigh
not brutally taken and cast aside;
like a beautiful aging woman

in her delicate decline
her beauty lies at such a depth
that it must be lived with a long time
until the superficial is seen right through
to the radiance within;

if you treat these pearls
like an indelicate swine
you will be momentarily satisfied
but never illuminated by the poem's
interior subtle delicate shine;

if a woman cuts 1 or 2 trees a year
from the forest at the foot of the mountain,
and burns everything carefully, she can
warm herself for the rest of her life and
never exhaust the Oak or the delicate Pine.

Honesty

If you want to see what real honesty is
look no further than the dog.
The dog doesn't give a damn for looking good

but will hunch the leg of the Queen's mother
if it feels like it. The dog
doesn't care what the hell you think, it will

lick its balls in the presence of the Pope
if that is what it has a mind to do.
The dog does not stand on position, power,

wealth or fame of any kind. He will
bite the rump of the Emperor if he
tries to pick up the dog's food; the dog

will lift its leg on the whitewall tire
of the Prime Minister's limousine or
shit on the Dalai Lama's prayer rug

because he is a dog and that
is what dogs do and
in some secret uncorrupted part of the self

we admire this honesty in dogs, because
we see it is absent in ourselves and
we know that such honesty

comes with a terrible price in this world.

Little Wind's First Book

Perhaps it was inevitable, given how much
we love one another, that my daughter would write books
like me, but it is real luck or maybe a touch
of the Guru's Grace that she writes true, hooks

to the gut with a sharp deadly punch,
and has a mean, angry, lean and hungry line.
She had to pay dearly for her skill, there's no free lunch
for any of us. Her heart was smashed just like mine

and yours by a world made for the breaking
down of the false in us, but there is no faking
it, either you write the truth or you are just
another loser left weeping in the dust.

Little Wind's first book has tremendous heart,
which means courage to speak the truth, the only human art.

The Supremacy of the Law of Sacrifice
(for Rick)

We are constantly receiving currents of gross energy
in the body, in the form of anger, joy, sorrow, fear
and other energies like them, live wire electricity
fed into the central nervous system where

we immediately assume it is about us, as in:
i am angry, or
i am afraid. We never consider that it is just passing
through us, holocaust, inferno, death, and we are

mere transformational units used to step up
the energy into a finer form which can then feed
our Creator. Instead of this sacrificial act, i keep up
the charade of self, stealing the energy out of my need

to suffer and horde,
refusing to feed our Lord.

The Range of Human Possibility

It truly makes me wonder Iain,
in this teeming, tempestuous broth of humanity
you were born into, which direction you will take.
Frost suggested but did not insist upon
the one the fewest people travel on but
Faulkner said it does not matter, it is all
a tale told by idiots like me and it means nothing.
Still, in every age known to man we have been given
living examples of what it can mean
to become truly human, not the mere
hint of humanity we see in ourselves when
we cannot resist the kind gesture,
the gently spoken word, but the full flowering
of the human being as in Buddha and Lao Tsu,
Krishna and Krishnamurti.
What a simple wonder we are grandson;
what miracle of Heaven could even imagine
that from the same gene pool could arise
Joseph Stalin,
who solved his problems by murdering others;
and Jesus, who
solved the problem of human ignorance
by allowing Himself to be murdered.
Whatever path you choose grandson,
remember this:
the only truly irresistible force is loving kindness;
though the sharpest stone may resist and resist, slowly
the water will wear it round and smooth.
i know this principle from my own experience

with your Grand Ma Chandrika who
by her loving kindness has made a surly,
fearful and disagreeable old idiot like me
acceptable in the company of human beings,
more or less.

The Great Wonder of This World

Grandson, one of the great wonders of this world
is your mother, who survived me, her mother and
her grandmother and as if that were not
suffering enough for an entire lifetime,
42 hours of labor delivering you.
Brilliant in her intelligence and
beautiful in her form, it was her laughter
which won my heart and changed me Iain.
i would do any stupid damn fool silly thing,
anything to make her and her sister laugh
and no one was ever more willing than they.
Oh how they loved to be tickled
as long as i stopped the moment they asked,
and i did.
That is perhaps the greatest wonder
this Earth has to offer my dear grandson,
laughter, and you have it in abundance;
a beast capable of the crucifixion of Christ
is able to laugh and when he does,
he is harmless. No one
ever hurt another while doubled over
in helpless laughter.
You can forget how to laugh my dearest,
i myself once did and it was thanks to your mother
that i remembered this simplest
of our Creator's blessings.
i believe it is through laughter
that we place ourselves in the company of angels;
the simplest definition of hell we ever need to know
is the absence of laughter.

Get Over It

I've got a new poem about my daughters,
about how like a God-damned fool
i broke their hearts and

after i read it this guy comes up to me
and says, Man you're still writing about
that; get over it.

That's a good one.
Only someone who has never done it or
someone who has and is so far gone

he cannot feel it, would believe
you can ever get over a thing like that.
It never goes away, it

tears and rips at the heart until
i am broken and ruined by it.
That is how men like me become

gentle and kind, utterly changed
by the angels of shame and remorse.
Some men destroy themselves; men like me

understand why but
we are the lucky ones, able to cover ourselves
in the rags of humility,

sewn by hand, piece by terrible piece
from the torn fabric
of our children's hearts.

The Sort of Fool i Am

i am the sort of fool any child can rule
without half-trying; i am dying
to love the little children, so above them
only in size but in every other way surprised
to find i am beneath. They are kind
and generous in their teaching. My reaching
after enlightenment seems absurd in the delight
of their climbing over my body, tickling sober
old foolish me until i laugh out loud, make ghoulish
faces and run races with them around the table.
i have one magic trick and the children grow thick
with happiness the more i repeat it. You can't beat it
finding an audience blind enough to be entertained
by a one-trick fool. Even when i go to their schools
the rules quickly evaporate in favor of exaggerated silliness
which they are more than willing to engage in until
we are all laughing and dancing as if this kind of romancing
could last forever. Never
do the children consider tomorrow, wherein all their sorrow
lies waiting; now, is all they are participating in
and they will let any fool like me play, and stay
as long as my silliness holds out, or the scolds
come around and sound the alarm:
Stop that foolishness, they say and in dismay
they retreat to their uncomfortable seats and i
put my clown nose in my pocket and look down
so the scolds can't see me smiling as i go piling
down the street in my clumsy stumble, a simple humble
fool loving children in a world cruel to them.

Opening the Gate of Power

i begin a poetry reading with drumming and singing,
which is called Opening the Gate of Power.
It is a blessing ceremony and i have learned
from doing it for many years that once it is done,
anything can happen, everything is possible,
because i am no longer in control, Power is.
Tonight i am reading at the Marsh Theater

in San Francisco. i have explained to them
that Power enters when called and
shifts the energy in the space.
i begin to read a poem about how we are
killing the animals and the terrible price
we must pay for doing so.
Just as i reach the part

where i am describing the slaughter of the animals,
right in front of me a little mouse
runs across the floor.
Not another poem, not another moment, but
just exactly at the moment the slaughter begins.
After that, i read the poem about young boys
bonding with women, their only hope.

With a miraculous exactitude only Power could generate,
my grandson Iain squeals at each appropriate moment,
only then, only this poem and no other.
Do not tell me your troubles; open wide that gate
and you will see that we are never alone and
everything you think you know
is wrong.

The Dharma Heart

Little Bear was a heavy, awkward boy
with as loving a Heart as you will ever find,
but our grade schools are the training grounds
for the social order,
which places no value at all on the Heart.

The social order is a pecking order
and its job is to find and expose
ruthlessly
every flaw you have and then
to exploit those flaws without mercy.

In his 6th grade teacher, Mr. Lavrov,
Little Bear found an angel but
in this world you have to pay
for every good thing you get.
Mr. Lavrov spotted Little Bear's Heart

and let him stand and read poetry
in front of the class.
One day he was reading before recess
and Mr. Lavrov left it up to him
when to dismiss the class

which began interrupting him
as the time for recess drew nearer.
This made Little Bear determined to finish,
another characteristic of his Heart,
and so he kept them 2 minutes over.

When he went outside for recess
they were waiting for him;
the whole class
including the girls
beat him mercilessly.

In a Dark Age such as ours
where poets are no longer admired nor read,
for a young boy to make such a stand
for poetry
is heroic and i confess

that Little Bear is a hero of mine,
the boy brave enough
to stand and read poems
while being set upon
by wolves.

Ordinary Madness

Just beneath the surface lives of ordinary people
lies a madness of such astonishing depth and power,
it is no wonder we destroy nearly everything we touch.
In one of the rooming houses my family once lived in,

down at the end of the hall lived a foul stinking man
and an ugly whore, both of them fat loud drunks.
We kids called them Stinky Pete and Gravel Gert.
Gert worked the streets at night and somehow brought home

a few miserable dollars from desperate ruined men.
Pete beat her regularly, their screams echoing in those dark halls
like the damned burning in the far reaches of hell but
Pete gave me something which made a difference for me.

You never know where help will come from. One day Pete
sat down beside me on the porch steps reeking of booze,
unwashed in a stinking undershirt and he said to me,
Stay away from the crowd, kid; nothing

is worth going with the crowd.
Somehow, i never forgot that. It helped me.
Even 2 or 3 people together are more of a crowd
than i can stand. i have been a loner all my life;

it has fed the hidden stream of the poems
which required long stretches of solitude
where i came to truly like the company.
Though i may die with a thousand regrets,

missing the company of others is not one of them.
i have never wanted for company, even of my own kind.
In solitude lies freedom:
no one to blame;

all responsibility begins there.

The Function of the Great and Famous
(Shallow Well Project: 618-997-5365)

He was once said to have the greatest promise
of any actor in our time and the fact is that
in a handful of roles he changed the face of acting
both for his generation and many to come, but

before he died, he became a terrible thing to see,
great beauty gone to monstrous fat, like
a sick walrus, a beached whale, a man
full of a longing that nothing could satisfy

except God and
that is the one diet he never tried.
Then there is one of my oldest friends;
as we grew up, the 2 of us had no promise

whatsoever. That absence of expectation
has allowed Tom to dare great things. He
spends 6 months each year in Africa where
he helps villagers install shallow wells

which save thousands of children who
die in large numbers from foul water sources.
It is good to see great men waste their foolish lives.
That creates a diversion so large that small men

like Tom can do great things and
no one gives them trouble or
gets in their way, nobody
even notices.

The Breeding Pen

A great Congress of the Saints of Heaven
was called 200,000 of our years ago
to solve a problem of universal consequence:

owing to the Work needs of the Great Creator
there had arisen a need for organic vessels
into which could be poured certain vibrations

useful to the maintenance of the Cosmic Machine,
but the creation of these organic vessels
had to be done voluntarily

as they were made to be destroyed
once they had been filled with vibrations,
this destruction releasing the resultant mix

of all the various vibrations put together.
And so the Saints of Heaven created
a cosmic Breeding Pen which they called

Gaia and they made it luscious, a garden
of sensual delight and in it they placed
Breeder stock who then

by their own initiative began to reproduce
the millions upon millions of organic vessels
required to be filled with vibrations

to maintain the Cosmic Machine.

The experiment succeeded beyond the most
exaggerated estimates of the Saints:

the Breeder stock reproduced in numbers
which astonished the most learned experts and
one very happy side-effect not predicted

by any of them was that the Breeders
began to destroy one another voluntarily
without intervention of the Saints.

These completely unexpected results
made everyone both above and below
very happy.

Languille and the Name of God

In spiritual practice when one has found a Guru,
the Guru's name is considered Sacred, one of the
names of God. The hope is held out that at death,
if one has practiced faithfully all her life
and dies with the Guru's name on her lips
as say, Mahatma Ghandi did with the name of
Ram, or Saint Joan with the name of Jesus, then

she will be liberated from the crushing wheel
of death and rebirth.
Naturally i have wondered, what if
the death comes suddenly, with such speed
that one has no time to collect one's thoughts;
what if
there is not time to think of the Guru's name?
Languille laid that fear to rest.

Languille was a French murderer,
sentenced in 1905 to die at the guillotine.
Dr. Beaurieux, the physician in attendance,
reports that immediately following decapitation
the eyelids and lips moved in rhythmic spasms
as he held the head in a cloth, then
the lids half closed so just the whites of the eyes showed,
just as he had seen so often in the dying and newly dead.
That is when he called out in a clear, strong voice,
Languille!

What he saw next he never forgot and

it haunted him the rest of his life:
the eyelids slowly opened without spasm,
then the eyes looked straight at him and
the pupils focused;
after several seconds, they slowly closed.
He called out again.

Again without spasm the eyelids lifted
and the pupils deliberately focused,
only this time it was different.
Dr. Beaurieux reports that the gaze
pierced his heart to his very Soul and
then closed slowly never to open again.

So i practice saying the Guru's name
over and over to myself during the day and
i remember Languille
who had no name but his own to recall
when everything counted on it and
his fate was being measured out
in the blink of an eye.

i Am the Guru's Boy

You can have your God and i am sure
He must be a fine fellow indeed
but i have used up all my means trying to cure
a broken heart and now i am in desperate need

of a friend who can steer me right
and bring your God down to where my feet
are standing on the ground; i am in a fight
for my life here and the Guru alone will not retreat

from my madness so i am the Guru's boy and
i have all my eggs in His basket. If He goes down
then i go with Him. There's a certain joy and
gamble in that, refusing ego's burning crown

for the Guru's slavery. All i have now belongs
to my Guru. He gets my credits, i eat my wrongs.

ix-xi

Small child plays on beach,
builds big castles, knocks them down;
tide is not concerned.

A Double Minded Man is Unstable in All His Ways
(James 1:8)

Blessed One, you who have the heart of your Father
in you, i come to you a troubled man, a man
of little faith, one who wavers and is beset with bother
in his heart so his faith is not stable. Rather than

a rock for a disciple, you have been given me,
a pebble which annoys the foot and makes it stumble
and upon which no sound thing is built. Doubt has driven me
to hide myself away in a fearful tremble

so no one sees this wretched disciple and by my sorrow
thinks You a fool as well Blessed One. i come torn,
a poor beggar, mind riven by yesterday and tomorrow,
to beg for surrender of my heart to the raging storm

of your love. All i have to offer is refusal to obey:
so great a gift, so poor the coin with which i pay.

Homeless Wandering Beggar

My only home is beneath the Guru's shawl
which is my sole refuge;
His Dharma clothes me and
His Sangha feeds me.

When the Guru's shawl is in motion
i move; when it is still
i am huddled beneath it.
There is no home but the Guru,

everything else is transient,
everything else falls down, crumbles,
becomes dust.
Only the Guru endures.

His Dharma is the shirt i wear,
i put on His Dharma like a pair of pants,
i place my feet in His Dharma,
i carry his Dharma like a begging bowl

which He is always filling up.
This Earth has ho home for me
but the Guru, who is my body,
my breath, my blood, my life.

Where there is a desert,
the Guru is the blowing sand;
where there is a mountain pass,
the Guru is the melting snow.

Do you understand that i have lost everything
and found the Guru? Do you not see
that i am nothing, that the Guru owns this
nothing and He makes of it what He wishes?

Come, fill my bowl with Your breath,
cover this flesh with Your garments,
lay Your dear hands on this brow,
let Your Grace rain upon this upturned face.

Part iv. The Master: The Angelic World

"At the end of the Way
The Master finds freedom
From desire and sorrow...

He wishes for nothing.
His food is knowledge.
He lives upon emptiness.
He has broken free...

He is the charioteer.
He has tamed his horses,
Pride and the senses.
Even the gods admire Him...

He cuts all ties.
He gives up all his desires.
He resists all temptations.
And He rises...

Honor the Man who is awake
And shows you the Way.
Honor the fire of His sacrifice."

— Buddha, *The Dhammapada*, 37–38, 152–154.

Born the King of Angels

If it is true, and
there are those who say it is, then
think what it means that
there lived somewhere in a place
we cannot even imagine, a Being
so advanced, so full of Light that
even the Angels

bowed down before Him and
called Him King and then
one day the call came:
You go down there
to the Ring of Suffering
and see what you can do, but

understand something:
it won't go easily for you;
no one leaves there unbroken.
What could He do?
He was the King of Angels

and He was not afraid so
He went
and He did good and so
they killed Him.

No one leaves the Ring of Suffering
unbroken.
Do not ask

for whom the Angels weep;
they weep

for us.

Sweet Things Turn Sour By Their Deeds

i have known women slim of ankle and fair of face
who by their deeds became their own disgrace.
i myself have shamed my dearest intention
by doing deeds of evil invention,
becoming that which i most hate
and succumbing to my basest fate.
We think that we are masters of our ship
but it is our fate which holds the whip
and we are mere puppets on the strings
unless we find a true Master who brings
with Him the means of our escape from the thrall
of our fate. By taking refuge beneath His shawl

we find the dearest hope of all mankind,
comfort for the weary, sight for the blind.

2 Women Breast Feeding

Mary and Beth sit at the dining room table
holding their new babies to the breast,
side by side like 2 strong Oak trees able
to hold up the sky while anchoring the Earth, the rest
of Creation falling humbly at their dear bare feet.
Give a human child the warm wet teat

for as long as he wants and he will not kill
or harm the Earth or others.
All of Creation depends upon breast feeding mothers
and if a child gets his fill
of milk from his mother's breast,
her gentle kindness will bring man's violence to rest.

Breast feeding women give God a sheer delight,
make Him feel momentarily that creating humans was right.

Awareness

Just as the unseen air
flows all around and
fills the empty pot,

so too does the mysterious unseen God
fill the body with breath
and become what we call

our life.
Pure Awareness is what we are;
we cannot be seen, yet

we fill the pot to overflowing,
permeate the breath of air and
cannot be contained.

The form does not endure,
the pot breaks,
the shards are cast aside,

become dust and
the air remains, invisible,
known only by its effect upon the dust

which stirs without a sound,
is moved and lifted by the air all around,
falls again silently to the ground.

Thank God for the Women
(for Mister Lee)

My daughters love me and treat me beautifully,
they are kind and forgive me though
i have made their hearts sore with my
clumsy ignorance and foolish hurtful ways;
thank God for the women.

My wife stood by me for 13 years. Though
i gave up on myself after my divorce and
my wounds made me afraid to love and commit
to the deep intimacy of marriage, she was
kind and forgiving; thank God for the women.

In my composition classes i ask my students to write
honestly about their fathers and mothers, both
their wounds and their gifts. The men often shy from this.
The women show them the way to their courage;
thank God for the women.

We are all Angelic Beings sent here to learn how to
love without restraint or defense or desire, the
common language of the Angelic worlds, but we
come here and are overwhelmed with the body's desires,
we lose our gentle kindness and our urge to forgive;

but women are asked to suffer the little children,
their arrogance is broken by childbirth, their selfishness
overwhelmed by a love they cannot name and they

carry this naked and vulnerable into the harsh world
as a flame to light the way for a tortured race

of broken and ruined Angels who have
forgotten who we are and
where we came from and
what we are sent here to learn; women are
the loving reminder of a kind and gentle God;

thank God, Oh thank God for the women.

For Chandrika, With Wonder & Gratitude

You will one day die, and it can only happen today,
whenever that particular today arrives as there is
only one day ever and that is always today,
so i am not complaining that you will die, nor
am i mourning such a personal loss as this,

though this particular loss will be far more for me
than my mother or father, and equaled only by the loss
of either of my daughters. No,
i am merely astonished and full of wonder to think that
this Earth could be without you my dearest and

still contain the likes of me. The most selfish prayer
would be that i die before you, but i do not pray that;
my prayer is that you die first, so that i might
in that one respect serve and care for you the way
that you have done for me our whole marriage.

i pray for the chance to see you through to the Light
which shines so clearly from your heart in a crown
about your head and form; i want to read aloud to you
from The Book of the Dead to make sure you are
alright and headed in the good direction once removed

from your gorgeous form which i will then burn and
cast its remains about your garden and into the compost
as you wish. No one else but me should do this because
i will do all of it with the deepest love i have known
and with a heart broken forever by love;

please Lord, let me be the last one standing, then
kneeling and weeping with wonder and
gratitude as the last ashes of love sift through
the first light dawning in her garden, the roses and
lilies covered in the thinnest film of her flesh.

The Sun For Whom This Curled Leaf Opens

She is gone away for 3 weeks to visit her mother when
the molar that hurts me so bad finally gives way, cracks
right down to the root and has to be taken out.

i come home to the empty house, scrub, peel, and chop
vegetables, steam them, process them into a broth
i can get down past the open bleeding hole, then

i go in and lay down on her bed, call her so i can
hear her voice and feel better.
Usually she is here to nurse me when i am hurting,

her kindness the only medicine i ever found which
could heal my broken heart once my daughters left.
Jesus fed the multitudes with a few loaves and fishes

and that was pretty good as far as Yogic powers go, but
she topped that without so much as a word of praise:
she made a craven coward brave enough to trust love;

she made a liar love the truth, a thief scrupulous
to the penny, a whore-chasing pimp unable to look
at another woman, a pornographer sickened

by the way they treat women.
Don't get me wrong, i love and admire Mister Jesus,
He was the genuine Master, the Adept Yogi, but

my wife makes me do good even when i am alone, she

compels me to go water the plants in her garden simply
by the force of her loving kindness.

You can kneel in your churches before your gods, but
i bow down before my wife's flower garden and
worship the ground she has tilled and planted,

hold the open petals in gentle hand,
cut the stems tenderly, bring them in,
place them in a crystal vase by her empty bed.

Natty Bumpo At the Waterfall

At 3 he is fiercely brave and wise,
two things we find intolerable, uncouth
because he will dare to tell the truth
in a world built on lies.

Natty Bumpo goes right to the waterfall's edge,
which is the way he lives,
picks up a stick and gives
it a heave over the ledge.

The Indians loved courage in a child, honed
and nurtured it by using the Earth
as the mother of self; born of woman, second birth
was from water, fire and stone:

he went into the Sweat Lodge a brave child,
emerged strong, stable, humble and utterly wild.

The Rain of His Grace
(for Will S.)

What's so special about my Guru, Mister Lee?
The answer's simple: He puts up with me.
The quality of His Grace is not strained
but falls upon me like a gentle rain
falls upon the petals in the gardens of heaven;
even for an arrogant fool like me it is given
freely on a daily basis.
Though my ignorance disgraces

me with its refusal to atone,
still i act as if, by my efforts alone
i could force the green bud to bloom
or the slumbering Soul to rouse from its tomb
of flesh. Can such a stubborn one as me
dear Master, ever come to you on bended knee?

The Lord and Owner of His Face

We are a mass of contradictions and of lies,
who cannot help doing what we despise.
Our every move is stolen from our past,
our feet move in the choreography of our vast
inheritance. Yet it is our faces
which most disgrace us,
for they are the masks of our conceit,
hide nothing, reveal our smallest deceit.

But my Master is One who owns His face,
is lord of His body and moves with conscious Grace.
In Him nothing is out of line;
He reveals what He wishes, otherwise no sign.
He was at Bridge when word came of His dear Master's death.
Three no-trump, He said. No sign, no wasted breath.

Come to God Dressed for Dancing

My Master sings lead in a bad ass Blues band;
He makes the choices very simple, either i come creeping
to God in a funeral procession and
surrounded by lamentations and weeping

or
i come like a whore
on payday, loud and prancing
my stuff, dressed for dancing,

coal black under my eyes, bracelets jangling
in a bawdy symphony;
my Master does not ever cry or beg for sympathy
but comes to God braided and tattooed, earring dangling

from one pierced lobe. There is no weeping in His abode;
His God is not a heavy load.

The Journals of My Master

His commitment is to make a journal entry every day
for 3 months and then to publish the results;
though there are many gems of Dharma

scattered about like diamonds in a field,
the real jewel is hidden right out in the open
where it cannot be seen.

Though the entries could be carefully edited
so they are polished and wise, though
they could be reworked so they are without error,

they are not.
What is more, there is no effort to censor His mind;
the result is that His mind is revealed to be

as sick and twisted and tortured as mine. This
is only part of the miracle however, because
this mind filled with trivial filth must be held up

against the demonstration of my Master's practice;
day after day and year after year
He never wavers in His practice, works

night and day, is patient beyond measure and
steady in His defense of the Dharma and yet
He has a mind like mine, not better or worse,

but just like mine and He reveals this

without pretense or face-paint. This
is the Pearl hidden in the journals

where all who have eyes to see may see
what it looks like in a human being when
the mind is no longer in charge.

The Value of Harsh Circumstances

Life in the roominghouses was harsh and
by the time i was 13, i was desperate
for a way out; this

drove me to Lee's Diner where i got a job
in the kitchen washing dishes next to Mister Lee,
whose wife ran the kitchen like a hysterical tyrant,

always yelling, screaming and cursing.
Everyone hated her and was afraid,
everyone but Mister Lee.

The thing i noticed eventually about Mister Lee
was that, unlike the rest of us, he
did not react to her, he

just kept doing what was
right in front of him. So one day
i asked him why he stayed with her.

It's a wise man who appreciates a tyrant,
he said, and he kept on washing the dishes.
Only he will seek out harsh circumstances;

the ordinary man will run from them
as fast as he can and he will lose their value.
How do you find a tyrant? i asked him.

You bait them with your life,

he smiled and kept washing the dishes.
If you do that, they will find you.

But what's the value of that? i wondered.
The Anasazi lived in Chaco Canyon 300 years,
he said. For them, the Canyon was

their tyrant,
as harsh a place as humans could find to live.
It reduced them to what was essential,

and once you find that inside, you become
an elemental force.
It focuses your Attention most wonderfully,

he said and she came storming through the door,
a tray of dirty dishes on her shoulder.
Goddamit Lee, clear me a place for these dishes,

she raged. He smiled at me and
kept on
washing the dishes.

The Umbrella

Mister Lee has come to His Father, Yogi Ramsuratkumar,
in Tiruvannamalai, India with
16 of His own disciples in hand.
He is accompanied as well by Purna,
His old disciple who is now a fine teacher
in His own right with students of His own.
And it is Purna I want to speak of here
for His own teaching demonstration
of a thing He learned from His Master, Mister Lee.

A group of male disciples is gathered
around Mister Lee
at the gate of Yogi Ramsuratkumar's ashram.
It is a dark day, pouring down rain
and the photographer is about to
take a picture of the scene.

The men are in various poses of slouch;
all eyes in the line of men,
including Mister Lee's, are
on the photographer, save one man's:
Purna.

Purna's eyes are looking straight ahead
and it is obvious why. He
stands next to Mister Lee and
without being obvious about it or
looking right at Him,
all of His attention is on His Master.

With His left hand in a painful
and awkward position,
He holds an umbrella over Mister Lee
who is smiling, peaceful and composed
next to His faithful disciple who is
soaking wet, in a painful position,
and utterly attentive
standing in an upright posture,
eyes alert and straight ahead.

It is clear that Mister Lee is pleased
and grateful.

The Sort of Master i Have

He is cruel to me, who
only wants to love Him; He denies me
this Grace and in its place

He gives me this terrible longing.
In this way i am like the brown rice
dumped hard and inedible in cold water.

As the heat rises the rice complains
that this heat is unbearable but
it longs to be food for the Master

so the faster the boil the softer
the rice grows until
it is asking for more so that

it can be proper food and feed
the sublime wonder of the Teacher.
Finally, when it is at its fiercest boil

its hard shell breaks down and
there is an explosion of softness within.
It makes a fit food for a Master to eat.

When everything appears to be moving faster
that is only me breaking down into softness,
preparing to leave this world.

I don't love this world

half so much
as where i am going.

Boil me in this longing dear Sir
and when i am done to your liking,
consume me.

My Master Touched My Face

One night i am waiting tables at a feast
and Mister Lee is at the head table.
It is a crowded room and someone asks me
to hand out the dessert forks.
i start at the head table and i bend over,
placing forks carefully by each person's place.

Mister Lee stops me and He
says to me, Just ask them
if they want a fork, it's not
so awkward. And then
right there in front of everyone He
reaches up with both hands and smiling,
He holds my face with a look of such
tenderness
that it breaks my heart.

Once Suzaki Roshi watched as 4 of His
strongest men worked with heavy sledges
to break up a boulder in His yard, smashing
and smashing but only every now and then
getting a chip.
Roshi stood there for awhile, then He
took a small hammer and walked
round the boulder, stepped up to it and

with a single swing He
split the stone in 2.
It is not the size of the hammer
but the perfect placement
of the blow.

The Impossibility of Being Human

Mister Lee that noble man, He works
without complaint night and day, 7 days
a week without rest, traveling the world,

India, Germany, France and He takes
small bands of His disciples with Him.
They tell how in India His foot got infected

so He went barefoot, limping from place to place
never slowing, never complaining; how
His body got sick, high temperature and He

never stopped, never saw a doctor, never
took anything, just kept on driving it,
serving His Father's work, talking

to people who cannot hear, radiant
before people who cannot see, always
dragging this Light impossibly towards us

while we cower in the terrible suffering
of our flesh and refuse, refuse
the only sane Love we will ever see.

Trapped in our blame and justification,
here He comes towards us, laying His life
down at out feet, suffering our crucifixion

without complaint.
How can we do otherwise than
to kill something like that?

The Murderer's Last Meal

Frankie Parker was a murderer,
on death row in Cummins prison where
he became a Buddhist practitioner,
a regular meditator, a Dharma dog.
He was an uneducated white boy in Arkansas
and plenty thought him retarded,
a moron.

So you could get good action
whatever label you wanted to bet on him.
When his time was up and
he had played his last card, they
came to him and asked him
what he wanted for his last meal.
Big piece'a pecan pie, big piece,
he said.

So the morning of his execution
they brought him a whole pecan pie
and a spoon.
He ate it slow, savored every bite,
one small bite every 5 minutes or so,
chewed and chewed tasting it
all the way down.

After a couple of hours
he called the guard over and told him,
Save this for me.
The guard looked and saw

Frankie had only eaten ½ the pie.
What do you mean, save it for you?
You're about to die.

I'll eat the other ½
after the execution,
Frankie replied.

Rain Drop Now is 30

She whom i sang lullabies to, sweet songs
of my own devising as i held her on our porch
in the summers of our laughter, now
is a kind and gentle woman, the sort
you rarely see in this or any age.

i am a stranger in her house of course,
an old man she once laughed with
and i know she would not hurt me
or anyone, she is too kind for that.
We forget how little kindness there is

in the world until we see it in someone like her
and then it is such a shock that i must sit down
and stare until i recover my breath.
i do not know where she came by such virtue but
i can tell you it did not come from me.

i am one with a cruel streak, love
does not come easily to me and kindness
is a thing i admire and aspire to but
it comes to me fitfully as the Moon will appear
briefly on a cloudy night and then

will be covered up again by darkness.
My daughter will look straight into my eyes
and sometimes we will hold one another for
moments at a time like that with our gaze and
my hand will rise like a Dove to her cheek

and all that is good in me comes forth then
and stands there in the light from her eyes.
She is an angel born into a world of sorrows
and i am her father, dumb with the luck
and the privilege of it, smitten with Grace,

my cold heart warmed by a kind daughter's face.

Learning to Obey the Master

One of Yogi Ramsuratkumar's disciples sings
beautiful devotionals in His Darshan. He
is 1 of 3 disciples who is not free
to mingle with the other devotees. Still he clings

to the idea that he can choose, so one day
when there was a big Guru celebration, all 3 of these
isolates decided to go to the gathering anyway,
even though they knew it would displease

their Master. Go wait in the house for me,
was all Yogi Ramsuratkumar said when they came
out among the huge crowds. To their horror and shame
the Guru spent the entire celebration sitting quietly

and uncomplaining, alone with the 3, who were broken
of their rebellion without a word being spoken.

The Triumph of the Skinny Man

You see a skinny little pencil-necked geek
like me and you think, He wouldn't have lasted
10 seconds in the old days, but
you would be wrong;

it was the skinny ones like me who
changed everything for the cave thugs.
The blunt, stony hunters and killers
just swung the biggest club they could find

and took their chances, but
the skinny man had to figure shit out
or get crushed and thrown away so
he figured shit out, like

while the thugs were bashing with clubs
the skinny man began to wonder
what would happen if this light-weight stick
was long and sharp on one end; or

everyone saw that if you dropped flint
on stone it made a spark but it was
a skinny man who figured out the
implications of that and

once he had a fire going a new class emerged,
not warrior but priest and
the skinny man became priest;
then he figured out how to pray.

Once there was prayer there was God
and the skinny man had power.
You might think that connecting to God
is the greatest thing the skinny man did

but you would be wrong there, too.
The brutes took what they wanted;
if they saw a woman they liked,
they took her

and brutally.
The skinny man didn't have a chance
against this brutality so
he wondered what it would take and

women, you owe it all to the skinny man,
so the next time you see one
be properly grateful because
it was the skinny man

who discovered the kiss.

The Guardians at the Gate

Today in the boneyard as i walked my daily rounds
across the street, 6 Crows lined up on the stones,
their dark eyes measuring my bones
for a possible fit beneath one of the fresh mounds

of shoveled Earth. Most days when i walk here
it is just me and the Crows in this recycling space.
The Crows know their place;
their job is to stand guard at the Dying Gate where

the newly dead Souls gather to be weighed.
On one scale the Crows place a single black feather
and the Soul climbs on the other.
The weight of our desires decides what must be paid:

desires tip, we go to hell; purgatory if they are even;
feather outweighs and Crows escort the Soul to Heaven.

Chopping Down Trees In My Back Yard

Sometimes you have to do the dirty work yourself
because it's right and the only way to do it, so
when my dear wife said we needed to take out
5 trees in our yard and suggested we get a friend
with a chainsaw to do it, i knew i had to do it,

by hand, with an axe and a saw, all alone;
if there was any tree killing to be done in our yard
it had to be me doing it, because i loved them
and they knew it.
It had to be my sweat and blood and hard labor

and suffering, a simple gesture of respect and
gratitude. These were not big trees, 3 with trunks
as big as my thigh, 2 as big as my upper arm. Still,
to take down a tree with an axe in 100 degree weather
is hard work especially if you don't love it;

if you do, it's a different level of labor.
First you pray giving thanks, this is the Indian way;
then you do a ceremony, a sign of reverence and devotion
which i did by walking around the trees chanting
the Guru's name; then you bow down and apologize

before going to the killing work.
If you don't love the trees this all sounds like bullshit;
if you do, this is the only way you can manage it and
feel you have done a right thing in a right way;
you make a gesture.

There is a lot to be said for a gesture, some small
sign of respect, a thing done with devotion.
In an age when murder of the Earth for profit is
the price of doing business, everything depends upon it.
Never mind changing others, never mind

waiting for others to do something, anything,
never mind looking for leaders;
on your knees alone in your own back yard
you sharpen the axe, sandpaper the head and
file the blade so it cuts cleanly, then

you begin,
like a man who puts down his own dying dog
rather than having the vet do it, not
as a skilled practitioner but as a lover,
with a broken heart.

This Path is the Dirt Road
(For Purna and Mr. Gold)

If you come to the Master's School to learn,
you will come away with nothing,
available help will remain hidden from you
and you will wither and fall away.

If you come to the School to work, to
Assist in the Master's Business, you will
in the course of this work learn some things,
perhaps flourish on the vine and even blossom.

Mister Lee once described those who come
only to learn and not to work; He said they
fail to practice,
think they are spiritual students yet

cater to the animal's every demand for comfort,
whine and complain,
are oblivious to School protocol and principles,
refuse to sacrifice petty desires

to build work energy,
think they are spiritual warriors. HA!
He said, standing in the rain and mud of India,
bus exhaust pouring in the windows, students

choking and gagging around Him. HA!
He said, and those who came to learn were
blinded by their own misery;
those who came to work,

worked in the dirt and the filth because
that is where the work is.
In order to find gold,
you have to get dirty.

Standing On the Bridge

i am standing on a bridge just now
made of peeled logs and two-by-fours
which spans a small creek.

It was made by an Eagle Scout
for his community-service project and
it is stout, thick and sturdy,

what you would expect of an Eagle Scout.
It is not like the great elegant spans
constructed by the geniuses

across the rivers and bays
of the continent, swaying over the
deep gorges and continental divides, those

wonders of the western world, but
i ask you, which one
would you prefer to be standing on

when the earthquake hits?

The Sex Gurus

Sooner or later it happens to all the Holy Men,
there is a sex scandal, we find out
He has been sleeping with the loveliest one
of His succulent nubile disciples and

that is the one thing we cannot tolerate
because we are so eaten up with it, so
starved for it and bottled up and filled
with rage and denial and wanting that

we cannot stand it that the Holy Man is
getting it from this young beautiful thing who
would not spit on the likes of us but
is laying down for Him, but I ask you:

who among you would deny her if she
came to you in the night bathed in her Holy flesh
and with one hand in your pants and
her tongue in your ear she professed

an uncontrollable love of God, who,
who among you would not urge her
to go to her knees in worship and begin
the righteous almighty speaking in tongues.

The Dangerous Prayer
(For Regina)

58 years i have done it all my own way
and it has led me nowhere. So now i pray
for you to break me
Master, take me

and make me your slave. Destroy
this self and turn me into your serving boy,
one who is given small, menial tasks
and leaps to assist when his Master asks

for some trivial thing. I pray dear Master
that you make me your footprint in the dust after
you have passed by; make me the sandals on your feet
so that i might always kiss your sweet

skin;
let shameless adoration be my only sin.

Respecting the Guru's Domain

There is a sense in which the Guru is owned
body and Soul by His devotees, a sense
in which He is their slave.
However, if this is true in any sense,
it is only true because the Guru
consents to it,

nothing else.
Ultimately, He is the only one among us
who is truly free.
So it shocked me and hurt me for Him
when one day i walked into the Guru's Ashram office
where He was set up behind a table
filled with Sacred bronze artifacts,
and i asked if i could speak with Him.

Of course, He said so i asked if i could
step around the table and enter the small
cramped space where He was sitting.
No, He said and then He looked
straight at me.

Thank you for asking, He said to me.
In all the years I have sat in this space,
you are the first person who
has ever asked me;
the only one.
Write a poem about that,
He said, so

that is what i am doing because
there is so little that can be done
to ease the suffering of a truly free man.

The Arising of All Creation Is Within

Mister Lee said, People are
always looking for something to enliven
them other than what they've been given

because what we've been given requires
consistency
and integrity,

which is challenging because
we want to let our Attention wander;
we want to squander

life, not deal with our own mind and feelings
in order to get to the root sensation
of the arising of all creation.

We have to pay and pay and pay
if we want the goods of The Way.

The Function of the Sangha Around the Master

Mister Lee said, In the beginning
the Master does
everything.

Slowly, people take over those
tasks of the Master.
This is how a community grows

in power.
This is the Law in every community. Based on
the community's ability, it will flower;

not on the community's wish to grow faster,
but on the community's ability
to free up the Master,

will the community flourish in Dharmic health
and be enriched in spiritual wealth.

He's All Business

The Guru sits up front on a platform
in a wide chair which is not like a throne,
it is a throne and

we go up and bow before Him,
bringing gifts like fruit and poems and
we leave them there at His feet but

that is not nearly enough,
He wants more; Give me
all your money, He says so

we buy everything He sells: books and tapes and
more bronze deity statues from India
than you can possibly imagine, tons of bronze,

boatloads, whole continents of bronze but
that is not nearly enough, He
wants more; Give me your obedience,

He says and many fall by the wayside
at this request, money is one thing but this
is different and still we give until it

hurts, though for most the very thought hurts,
and then He saves the best for last because
it is the hardest, nearly impossible; Give me

your suffering, He says and they leave

in droves, the roads leading to hell
are bumper-to-bumper day and night.

Give me all you've got, everything,
He says, a big smile on His face, And
I'll see what I can do for you;

I know some people.

Just Follow

To follow is the
easiest thing in the world,
Mister Lee said to a group of disciples
gathered around Him.
Why don't you
just follow?
I love to follow, He continued.
It is the most easeful,
peaceful thing to do. Instead
you have all your opinions,
ideas,
your needs. Go here,
do that, do this,
requests,
I need, I want,
always trying to
control
everything.
It's terrible,
He said and
for a moment the disciples
grouped around Him were silent.

Then one of them spoke up; Why
don't we go over there for chai?
No, not there, another said,
it's too crowded.

Madness Cannot Stand My Master's Face

Master, you have completely undone me,
torn me from my comfort zone of dreaming
and pretending, lying and constant scheming;
all the old tired tricks that used to run me

lost their charm
once i saw the honesty of your simple grace.
Dear Master, i suffer to look into your face
because i see reflected there the harm

i do to self and others by my selfish lazy
ways; though they still have power to seduce,
i can no longer use ignorance as my excuse
for being crazy.

Serving you, i can't dance to the same old tune;
better to try emptying the ocean with a spoon.

Most People Just Go Crazy

We have all lost our courage, lost
whatever it was we came in with that gave every
one of us our edge and made us unique. The cost
of fitting in is that we forfeit our bravery

and replace it with self importance and self pity.
We go crazy but it is an imitation, shallow and cheap
which never works for us because it lacks integrity
of the kind my Guru demonstrates, a deep

original craziness stabilized with wise innocence.
Once i was shocked to see Mister Lee in a crowd,
fiercely human in the common herd; without defense
He stood in their midst, as still and present as they were loud

and lost. i think my ordinary madness a clever disguise,
but it lacks style, is merely vulgar next to the crazy-wise.

We Wake Up Empty and Afraid

Every day it is the same thing:
before we can assemble our ordinary face
the Soul stands there trembling,
naked and alone, without a trace

of knowledge; having no clothes of its own,
it is dressed in emptiness.
Friend, escape into the Tavern of the unknown
before the door closes. Never mind your dress,

all who sit here are naked before
the company of the Saint; He is the thief
of Hearts so why be afraid? Adore
His cunning, admire His skill. Your belief

that you own something only brings you grief;
the tree does not fear the wind which steals its leaf.

The Bardo of Loneliness

Beloved i am so far from you just now,
lost in the bardo of loneliness,
a city within, which does not allow
you to enter;

they lock the gates when you come and
oh my dear without you it is
so unspeakable a madness.
There is laughter all around but

no joy in it.
They pour the wine, they
set out the food, they light the pipe
but nothing satisfies.

Without you, the leaves grow yellow and fall
and the birds no longer sing, their call
such a far off echo in the empty sky.
Oh my Beloved i do not want to build my house

in the poisons of the ruined garden.
Where is your touch here, where, where
your sweet voice; come to me dearest, please
come and lead me from these streets of sorrow

into your quiet temple.
No more the loud denial,
no more the turning from your shining.
All that lives here moves,

but does not shine.

Drink From the Presence of Saints

Every drunk has his favorite wine.
The Saint Anjenaya is mine;
His grape is the sweetest on the vine.

In His Tavern we drunkards play
waiting for the Lord to take us away,
waiting for Anjenaya's gaze to slay

our sobriety.
We drunks are the outcasts of society,
reviled by our Master's notoriety.

We are lost and beyond caring,
each night in His Tavern sharing
His overflowing cup and shamelessly staring

at His beautiful form.
For one sip from His lips i will risk the world's scorn.

The Hidden Yogi

Some of the greatest enlightened Masters die unknown.
Hell, one may be buried across the street in the bone-
yard where i walk among the Souls in the evening gloom,
winter breath gathered about me like impending doom.
You can have your Krishna, your Buddha and your Christ

but i will take the one who worked the kitchen, diced
potatoes so fast and thin it is said His hands were a blur
and the apprentices gathered around just to watch Him stir
a roux or blend a tender sauce with wine
and though He seldom spoke, they remembered every line
because His patient kindness was wisdom without showing.
By skillful means He roused their inner muted knowing.

The Hidden Yogi works unnoticed in the crowd,
pierces the heart then moves on toward darkness, head bowed.

Rain Drop's Subtle, Hidden Art

Right from the start
she understood the miracle of the human Heart,
how it was not merely an electro-chemical pump for blood
but was an instrument of subtle power, like a flood
hidden in the first drop of rain.

Unlike most, she was not totally seduced by her brain
so that she lost all touch for her feeling
and succumbed to the brain's brazen stealing
of the energies of love for its own reason.

Of course she endured a dry and lifeless season
in her youth, one where the madness ran wild;
still she recovered quickly her strong but mild
inner life. It is easy to miss her depth of power,
like the raging torrent concealed in the first gentle shower.

Shirley

The frail black woman who cleaned our house, Shirley
was also the silent witness to the squalor of
our lives, to the ruin of my mother and father
thrown without compass or rudder
onto the raging tormented sea of booze
from which they never found a landfall
or even momentary port in the storm.

She was impossibly kind to my sister and i,
lost and abandoned in the wreckage
of our parents. She nurtured
and befriended us, bought us small
delicate gifts from her meager salary but
it was her heart which won the trust
of a feral tortured suspicious boy and

made me walk with her each day
to the bus stop, holding her hand until
the neighbors spoke of it and
my father whipped me until i stopped.
Years later, home on college vacation,
i spotted the frail bent shadow moving
along the street from cleaning job to bus stop and

i stopped the car, got out and went to her.
Her eyes lit like the candles in a cloister and
she put her dear arms around me, whispering
my name. That was in the 60s in a segregated
Illinois town and every time i went to the streets

and the barricades and the police in the name of
the civil rights of men and women,

it was her i risked it all for,
for the kindness in her touch and her eyes when
all around me the dark sea of human grief
tore at the shores of the heart. When
i was a small boy, sitting quietly in church
and heard the 23rd Psalm: Surely
goodness and mercy shall follow us

all the days of our lives, i thought
they were talking about
her.

King Snake

We say the Snake is the lowliest of creatures and
as a sign of derogation and contempt we
call a man a snake but
we have it all wrong,
upside down and backwards
as usual.

The Snake is a Kingly creature,
by its very nature commanding
the highest regard and respect
from every living thing.
I am camped deep in the forest
and today I hike along Snake Creek

headed for the Tall Grass Meadow
when I come to a lovely stretch of creek
with a nice 6 foot spit of pebbled beach
so I head down through the trees for it,
making my way carefully because
it is Snake season.

They do not say it is human season
because they are not afraid of us,
but just the time of year we know they are
out there
makes us tremble with respect, the way
the lowliest peasant trembles before a King.

There on the pebbled beach

lying splendidly in the Sun
is a Copperhead,
big one,
3-4 feet uncoiled
and my body leaps back

the way a courtier does who
rounds a corner and comes
face to face with the King.
He turns His head slowly toward me,
unmoving and unafraid,
the Sun dappling His brown and yellow body

and everything giving Him
royal space; even the bugs
who swarm around me
do not come near Him.
There is around Him a field of force
which radiates for many feet in all directions

the way it does around a King who
enters a room and everyone bows because
He has the power to kill them at will
and they know this and even the humans,
those lowliest of creatures,
respect this.

A Bunch of Morons

i work in a university with men and women
who are all experts in their field; they
think they know something.
They have thought about it all,
read the books, written the papers,
gone to conferences,
taken good notes and
formulated satisfactory conclusions, but

there is one idea
which seems to give them
an extraordinary amount of
difficulty
which is the idea that
we are all, every one of us,
a bunch of morons.
They cannot seem to grasp this

simple and obvious fact about
every single one of us and
it got me to wondering about
the whole notion of what genius is.
Then i remembered Socrates, one of
the great Masters of His or any time,
who said, I only know one thing:
that I know nothing. Now there

is a real moron for you.

The Way of Faith

We are foolish little people easily seduced
by habit and subject to unlimited fears;
forgetting that we come from God, we are reduced
to maggot food and drown in foolish tears

of guilt and loneliness. So the great Power
sends us reminders of who we are in the guise
of Masters, and when people see them they cower
and say, There's a crackpot. But Masters are crazy-wise:

Once in the blazing heat of summer Swami Samarth went
to the house of His devotee asking for cool water;
she was horrified because her well was dry and she rent
her veil in anguish. Swami laughed and said, Come daughter;

He went outside and peed beside her empty well;
at once it filled with water in a graceful rising swell.

Master Xu-Yun's Teaching On Mercy

In his 112th year Master Xu-Yun
presided over Yun-Men Monastery
and 120 monks. That year 1952
a band of more than 100 Red thugs
surrounded the monastery looking for
gold, silver, and arms which rumor said
were hidden in the temple;

they searched high and low for 2 days
from the roof tiles to the floor bricks.
Finding nothing they locked Xu-Yun
in a bare room lit by a single lamp with
no food or water.
He was forced to shit and pee on the floor.
On the 3rd day ten thugs entered

and demanded the treasures.
When he said that he had none
they beat Xu-Yun with wooden sticks,
then with iron bars until
his head and face were covered with blood
and his ribs were broken.
All the while he sat in the meditation posture;

they beat him 4 times that day then
left him for dead. His disciples
carried him to bed and helped him sit
in the meditation posture.
On the 5th day the thugs found him still alive

and they were furious, beat him with wooden sticks,
kicked him and trampled him with heavy boots.

Laughing, they left him for dead.
Again his disciples carried him to bed
and helped him sit in the meditation posture.
On the 10th day he appeared to lay there dead but
his body was still warm so 2 of his disciples
kept watch by his bedside.
On the 11th day he sat up.

The thugs who beat him saw this and
began to whisper among themselves;
they grew afraid.
Their leader asked Xu-Yun
why he did not die from the beatings.
He said he wanted to spare them the bad karma
they would incur for killing him.

The men began to tremble and
were never seen in those parts again.

Satchel Paige

A good argument can be made that
he was the greatest pitcher who ever lived and
one of the cornerstones of that argument

would be what happened in 1942
when the greatest hitter in Negro League history,
Josh Gibson, faced the greatest pitcher, Satch.

Paige was skinny with legs as long as Pine trees
and Gibson had a barrel chest and shoulders
2 yards wide, thickly muscled hams for biceps

and his menacing crouch at the plate was feared
by every pitcher in the game save one: Satchel;
he wanted Josh

and in that historic game he
wanted him bad enough that he
walked 2 men to fill the bases so he

could pitch to Josh and then
he called out to the greatest hitter in baseball
exactly what he was going to throw and

struck Gibson out
on 3 straight
pitches;

a good argument
can be made and
that was Satchel's argument.

Haydn Didn't Give A Shit If You Liked the Work

It is easy to put off the impulse to write
out of fear or laziness, the fear being mainly
that i am not good enough, that no one

will like what i write, that i cannot do it
anymore or that i never could, that i have nothing
that anyone would want to read, and then

there is the laziness which is just fear
wearing a cheap suit.
i have known many who said they were

poets or writers of one kind or another and
occasionally they put something down on paper
but it had no suffering in it, it had not

been properly paid for, 10 false starts
for one good beginning, 10 lousy poems for
one worth fighting for, struggling with, beginning

again and again until you get it right.
Franz Josef Haydn wrote 104 symphonies, some of them
were not much to listen to i will grant you, but

goddam! There were 104 of them.

Just Beyond the Magpie's Song, the Hungry Shadows Loom

Goya was an artist who took great risks but
he was very intelligent about it; a master
of his craft, he exaggerated certain
of his subject's features to reveal
truths about their nature which
were not flattering

but most were so dull-witted and his fame so great
that the nobility he painted dared not complain.
One of the paintings i admire most is
Don Manuel Osorio de Zunuga,
a portrait of a spoiled, ruined little prince
dressed in ruffles and bows and lace

holding a string tied to a magpie's leg.
The child's eyes are blank ciphers of loss
and dead innocence but they are not the eyes
which dominate the painting,
those belong to the 3 cats
crouched mainly in shadow at the prince's feet.

They are crouched the way cats do just before
they leap and tear their prey and
their eyes are fixed in a wide murderous stare
on the magpie on a string who
strolls before them, safe only in the prince's presence,

before whom they dare not leap.
The black cat is enveloped in shadow, only

his yellow eyes visible like 2 burning coals but
the brindle cat is fully lit and his eyes are mad
with intention, he means to kill. The little prince,
who momentarily has the world on a string, is

lost and oblivious, you can see it
in his eyes; he is unaware that just behind him
the fang and the claw await and
the string of power and privilege is an illusion
that cannot save him. He does not yet understand
the limitations of power;

the cats do.

The Master Luthier's Advice to His Young Apprentice
(for René Morel)

What is wanted and needed is skill, feelings,
and concentration.
In the absence of experience,
deep feeling is called for, an outpouring
of the most impossible tenderness

because she must be opened; even
so fine a cello as the Countess of Stanlein*
must be opened; your caress
must be ever so delicate
in order to bring a complete full sound
from her throat.

Once she is opened
you have to be patient, give it time;
you must have a way with the flesh
of the finger, the vibrato of the hand.
She must be delicately moistened

in order to make her more malleable.
It cannot be hurried, must
never be rushed: you insert your instrument
carefully, carefully, just here
into the glue—you must
know how to do it—and then

you just go pop!
Every touch must be unforced,

the strokes soften
but do not penetrate too deeply and
the desired end is always sonority.

* The name of a Stradivarius cello

What it Takes to Write the Good Poems

The best poets have dirt under their nails
and are bent from the 8-hour day.
The rest are empty sails
unable to catch a good wind or even stay

afloat on a calm sea.
Hard labor makes honest men
and it gives the line a ferocity,
an inner strength so it will not break when

placed under extreme duress.
The world is full of poets who crack
when asked to endure the stress
of a heavy load carried on the back.

A tired man writes a simple unadorned line;
there are no flowers in factory, loading dock, or mine.

The Myth of Great Talent

The illusion is, great talent always rises to the top.
You only had to know Debbie Snow to stop
believing that. The finest singer i have ever known,
she sang in New York subways for dimes and got bone
cancer at 32, died in 3 months. When i hear her voice
on tape something in me is restored every time and i rejoice
that such a singer ever lived on Earth.

The only Grace is finding your art, the only worth
is remaining true to it, nothing more.
Whether you live the life of a saint or a whore
does not matter, no one is spared, no one gets out alive.
Great talent may just as often starve as thrive,
while mediocrities grow rich in every field;
so follow your art to the end and never yield.

The Only Grace is Bad Poetry

I used to think that Shakespeare was about
as good as it can get in English poetry.
Then i ran into Charles Bukowski,
a bum of no merit in the pecking order,
a man whose only claim to greatness was
he told the truth, no matter how bad
it made him look and
all of a sudden my ideas of what constituted
greatness in poetry were in ruins.

But i did not count on meeting up with
that bad poet Mister Lee.
Mister Lee is as bad a poet as any who
ever lived and i stand in His lineage.
i stand on His shoulders.
He is the foundation upon which
we bad poets stand.

I once was a good poet, many said so
and i competed for the biggest prizes but
it was no damn fun, no good for me.
Now, thanks to my dearest Master,
i write this dreadful drivel,
because i cannot praise Him enough
nor stop speaking of what He does for me
inside where no one can see.

Dearest, you have performed a miracle
and the only way i can let people see it

is to allow you to make me a bad poet
just like you.
I adore this bad poetry which
throws itself on its face in the dust
at your dear, Beloved feet.
Anyone can be a good poet, but
poetry this bad comes by Grace alone.

The Bad Poet Sings

It comes as a profound shock to me that
i spent all of my adult life training,
working night and day, studying,
reading, writing all the damn time
to be a really good poet, no that is
not right, to be
the finest poet who ever lived and

yet after 45 years of effort it was
obvious to me that at my best i was
second-rate and that was at my best;
so it comes as a profound shock to me
that i am the apprentice to the Master,
the finest Bad-Poet in this world and
it is bad poetry, bad poetry mind you

which is His Path to God,
not good poetry, never mind great poetry,
i am in training to be a bad poet.
Lord have mercy upon my second-rate heart
i had it all wrong for most of my life.
Instead of fighting to improve i should have been
giving up and getting worse.

I have seen how the best poets who ever lived
all went nowhere, did not develop the Soul
but the talent instead and
they were left bereft of inner virtue,
without a clue where wisdom lay.

You read their line and though it be pretty,
it is hollow and empty of wisdom.

And now i cannot even be the finest bad poet
who ever lived; my Guru is the King of the
Bad Poets and i serve at His whim,
i sing His praises in every line and breath:
Bow down and worship the Great Fool, the
Lord of Bad Poets. This one is for your dear Sir;
it doesn't get any worse than this.

Hearing With the Guru's Ears
(for R.S.R.)

She writes to tell me that my poem to the Guru
is a love poem, and it made her weep.
This is a shock to me, i thought it was
a complaint,

the unfulfilled cry of longing
from one unfit for love.
Is it possible that the broken reed
plucked from the tangle along the riverbank

is made into an instrument of delight
and does not even know it;
who plays this hollow bamboo,
what breath makes such subtle music

that the flute does not hear its own singing?
It has only the voice, but the Guru has
the ears to hear the sweet melody
hidden in a symphony of regret.

One Way to Love God

Perhaps there is an easier way to it
but most poets don't know how to do it
other than writing their way to the bone,
the long terrible labor done alone
to tell the truth no matter its pain,
and hard work done for love of the line, not gain
of any kind.
Eventually the faithful poet can find

her way to something holy
if she has patience. If she works slowly
to perfect the craft the miracle arises
on its own: perfection of the self, all its disguises
torn away
as she surrenders to her art and is borne away.

Li Po at the River's Edge

Fifteen centuries ago in China
lived a poet named Li Po who loved
to sit by the river in the evening,

drink wine which he loved and
write poems in his notebook
which he loved even more, then

tear out the page
and make a little paper boat,
set it on fire

and let it float down the current
until it sank.
Some nights a whole string of boats

on fire with the music
blazed a trail downstream,
setting fire to the world;

some nights a lone blazing verse
set forth into the dark
on fire with a single spark

of inspiration;
and some nights the sultry dark
pressed down upon the sullen water

in a seamless dreaming, no fire,

no sound except the rice wine
gurgling in the throat

of the bottle and
every now and then
a soft, rich, satisfied laugh,

no light,
not even an ember,
to mark his way home.

Let the Work of the Potter Teach You

With her foot she turns the wheel
and turns upon it, on the spinning clay
she spins the clay, combines
form and formless, water joined
with clay to make a shape

to hold emptiness.
Always working with 2 things, she becomes one:
between thumb and finger a shape appears,
between water and clay a fire,
between form and emptiness

the bowl is filled with water;
she takes it to her lips;
between longing and thirst,
the satisfying drink.

The Wise Man's Wisdom is Often Hidden
(for Hayden)

In this world, wisdom is not valued half
so much as bullshit;
the cheap laugh
is much preferred over wit.

I once heard of a great saint
who lived for years on the town garbage heap
and never once voiced complaint.
Most wise men keep

quiet,
not because they wish to hide
anything, but simply because there's a riot
of noise made by human pride

which makes the very air corrupt
and the wise man does not wish to interrupt.

All Done Grando

If the Earth is the theater of cruelty, then
humans are the puppets who dance upon its stage,
pulled first this way and then that by forces
hidden in the shadows of sorrow;
what god lifts this hand, what demon places it
upon your brow?
Everyone suffers, every living thing here suffers, the tree,

the brook, the still pond at the mountainís foot, and
of course you and me, but only those among us
untouched by madness,
only the little children of all ages can see what force it is
which lifts the hand.
Take Iain, my Grandson who is 2 and
calls me Grando; one late afternoon

we stood on the screened porch,
ready to go for a walk in the boneyard and when
i opened the screened door a stray cat from the neighborhood
darted from the bushes past my foot and in through the door.
Without thinking, half in rage, half in fear, i slammed the screen
trapping its body between wooden door and concrete step.
It howled and i shouted at it to get out.

Iain stood there transfixed, no psychic veil
between him and the cruelty of the dance; at 2 he
still sees with the whole body thanks to his mother who
has not robbed him of his organic goodness so
he remains rooted and steadfast in the real world.

Just that fast i broke momentarily with his goodness and
he knew it.

When i turned to him for his hand, he
took one tiny but decisive step back,
eyes wide
as 2 stars blazing in a darkened sky and
that fast his trust in me
was momentarily gone;
All done Grando,

he said and turned
to seek his motherís arms,
not mine.
If we are given a single moment of light
like that in a lifetime of drowning in shadows, then
maybe it is possible for something to be reborn in us,
something inhuman but not unkind. However,

first the old lies must die,
they must go
the way of the yellow leaf,
in their place a heart
broken with innocence,
radiant with grief;
anything else and

Iain will not play.

Epilogue:

We Own Nothing, But Are Owned

We Own Nothing, But Are Owned

Do not praise the writer of these songs
but praise the One to whom the poem belongs;
we are lonely here, but not alone,
know nothing, but are known.
The One who knows writes everything we read,
takes each breath, fulfills our every need.

So when you praise be sure you understand
the poem is not a product of the poet's mind;
though it comes from the labor of the poet's hand,
its source is as the light is to the blind:
unseen but felt, a subtle sense which guides and
moves without forcing, is both wise and kind.

If there is merit in this verse,
place the coin of praise in the Maker's purse.

THE WAY OF POWER
by RedHawk

"This is such a strong book. RedHawk is like Whitman: he says what he sees..." – the late William Packard, editor, *New York Quarterly*.

"Red Hawk is a true poet whose work has strong, credible feelings and excellent timing." – Richard Wilbur, U.S. Poet Laureate and Pulitzer Prize winner.

"This collection continually surprises with insights that sometimes stop the breath." – Miller Williams, winner of 1995 Academy Award of the Academy of American Poets.

Paper, 96 pages, $10.00   ISBN: 0-934252-64-5

THE ART OF DYING
by RedHawk

RedHawk's poetry cuts close to the bone whether he is telling humorous tales or indicting the status-quo throughout the culture. Touching upon themes of life and death, power, devotion and adoration, these ninety new poems reveal the poet's deep concern for all of life, and particularly for the needs of women, children and the earth.

"An eye-opener; spiritual, native, populist. RedHawk's is a powerful, wise, and down-home voice." – Gary Snyder

Paper, 120 pages, $12.00   ISBN: 0-934252-93-9

To order: 800-381-2700
Or, visit our website at www.hohmpress.com

AS IT IS
A Year on the Road with a Tantric Teacher
by M. Young

A first-hand account of a one-year journey around the world in the company of *tantric* teacher Lee Lozowick. This book catalogues the trials and wonders of day-to-day interactions between a teacher and his students, and presents a broad range of his teachings given in seminars from San Francisco, California to Rishikesh, India. *As It Is* considers the core principles of *tantra*, including non-duality, compassion (the Bodhisattva ideal), service to others, and transformation within daily life. Written as a narrative, this captivating book will appeal to practitioners of *any* spiritual path. Readers interested in a life of clarity, genuine creativity, wisdom and harmony will find this an invaluable resource.

Paper, 725 pages, 24 b&w photos, $29.95   ISBN: 0-934252-99-8

NOBODY SON OF NOBODY
Poems of Shaikh Abu-Saeed Abil-Kheir
Renditions by Vraje Abramian

Anyone who has found a resonance with the love-intoxicated poetry of Rumi, must read the poetry of Shaikh Abil-Kheir. This renowned, but little known Sufi mystic of the 10th century preceded Rumi by over two hundred years on the same path of annihilation into God. This book contains translations and poetic renderings of 195 short selections from the original Farsi, the language in which Abil-Kheir wrote.

These poems deal with the longing for union with God, the desire to know the Real from the false, the inexpressible beauty of creation when seen through the eyes of Love, and the many attitudes of heart, mind and feeling that are necessary to those who would find the Beloved, The Friend, in this life.

Paper, 120 pages, $12.95   ISBN: 1-890772-04-6

To order: 800-381-2700
Or, visit our website at www.hohmpress.com

RUMI ~ THIEF OF SLEEP

180 Quatrains from the Persian
Translations by Shahram Shiva   **Foreword by Deepak Chopra**

This book contains 180 translations of Rumi's short devotional poems, or *quatrains*. Shiva's versions are based on his own carefully documented translation from the Farsi (Persian), the language in which Rumi wrote.

"In *Thief Of Sleep*, Shahram Shiva (who embodies the culture, the wisdom and the history of Sufism in his very genes) brings us the healing experience. I recommend his book to anyone who wishes *to remember*. This book will help you do that." – Deepak Chopra, author of *How to Know God*

Paper, 120 pages, $11.95   ISBN: 1-890772-05-4

THE MIRROR OF THE SKY
Songs of the Bauls of Bengal
Translated by Deben Bhattacharya

Baul music today is prized by world musicologists, and Baul lyrics are treasured by readers of ecstatic and mystical poetry. Their music, lyrics and accompanying dance reflect the passion, the devotion and the iconoclastic freedom of this remarkable sect of musicians and lovers of the Divine, affectionately known as "God's troubadours."

The Mirror of the Sky is a translation of 204 songs, including an extensive introduction to the history and faith of the Bauls, and the composition of their music. It includes a CD of authentic Baul artists, recorded as much as forty years ago by Bhattacharya, a specialist in world music. The current CD is a rare presentation of this infrequently documented genre.

Paper, 288 pages, $24.95 (includes CD)   ISBN: 0-934252-89-0
CD sold separately, $16.95

To order: 800-381-2700
Or, visit our website at www.hohmpress.com

FOR LOVE OF THE DARK ONE: Songs of Mirabai
Revised edition
Translations and Introduction by Andrew Schelling

Mirabai is probably the best known poet in India today, even though she lived 400 years ago (1498–1593). Her poems are ecstatic declarations of surrender to and praise to Krishna, whom she lovingly calls "The Dark One." Mira's poetry is as alive today as if was in the sixteenth century—a poetry of freedom, of breaking with traditional stereotypes, of trusting completely in the benediction of God. It is also some of the most exalted mystical poetry in all of world literature, expressing her complete surrender to the Divine, her longing, and her madness in love. This revised edition contains the original 80 poems, a completely revised Introduction, updated glossary, bibliography and discography, and additional Sanskrit notations.

Paper, 128 pages, $12.00   ISBN: 0-934252-84-X

ORDERING, SHIPPING AND HANDLING INFORMATION:

Surface Shipping Charges:
1st book $5.00
Each additional item $1.00

Shipping Methods:
Surface U.S. Mail—Priority   Fedex Ground (Mail + $3.00)
2nd-Day Air (Mail + $5.00)   Next-Day Air (Mail + $15.00)

Method of Payment:
* Check or M.O. Payable to Hohm Press, P.O. Box 2501, Prescott, AZ 86302
* Call 1-800-381-2700 to place your credit card order
* Call 1-928-717-1779 to fax your credit card order

To order: 800-381-2700
Or, visit our website at www.hohmpress.com

About the Cover

Entreaty

Old Ones grow their architecture and their magic from the seeds of stony circumstances and the forces of their land. The complexity and ingenuity of their mythology molds the mechanisms of social control and the answers to personal invocations. The evidence is in the land. The culture is an organism growing into a veiled system for survival, first answering the land's demand and then expanding into a pattern that takes on a life of its own. The man-of-the-land's reverence for the sun, his allegiance to the raven, and his sworn secrecy of the kiva become hidden motives, obscure ceremonies, and sacred laws. Aesthetics, politics, and sociology all roll into one mysterious canon.

– Gary Simmons, cover artist

• • •

Gary Simmons is known for his virtuosity with pen and ink, a medium he taught for Rapidograph Pens in their national workshop program. He has written *The Technical Pen: Techniques for Artists* and produced an educational video, *A Pen-and-Ink Demonstration by Gary Simmons.* Gary is best known for his draughtsmanship and his highly accomplished pen-and-ink drawings of a broad range of subject matters. He has executed a wide variety of large portrait montages, western subjects, equine scenes, nudes, landscapes, animals, and mythology, including several series based on Leda and the Swan.

In addition to the pen-and-ink medium, Gary has worked in

terra cotta sculpture, pastel, lithography, oil paint and watercolor. He has recently begun concentrating specifically on the combination of watercolor and ink as well as oil painting. He has taught art for Henderson State University since 1991. He has been awarded the Arkansas Arts Council Governor's Award for Individual Artist and was honored by the Arkansas Advertising Federation 2004 Distinguished Educator Award. His studio is in Hot Springs, Arkansas where he lives with June, his wife of forty-one years and the mother of his two daughters, Jamie and Rebecca.

Contact Info:
penman@cablelynx.com
Studio: 501-525-1639
133 Brown Drive
Hot Springs, AR 71913